Nathaniel Hawthorne
and the Tradition of Gothic Romance

By

JANE LUNDBLAD

HASKELL HOUSE
Publishers of Scholarly Books
NEW YORK
1964

First Published **1946**

HASKELL HOUSE PUBLISHERS Ltd.
Publishers of Scarce Scholarly Books
280 LAFAYETTE STREET
NEW YORK, N. Y. 10012

Library of Congress Catalog Card Number: **65-15898**

Haskell House Catalogue Item # **589**

Printed in the United States of America

CONTENTS

"He lives in an American Gothic world."
Professor Harry Levin in *The Quintessence
of Hawthorne*. *The New York Times Book
Review*. June 16, 1946.

"We do not remember to have seen any translated specimens
of the productions of M. de l'Aubépine — a fact the less to
be wondered at, as his very name is unknown to many of his
own countrymen as well as to the student of foreign literature.
As a writer, he seems to occupy an unfortunate position between the Transcendentalists (who, under one name or another,
have their share in all the current literature of the world) and
the great body of pen-and-ink men who address the intellect
and sympathies of the multitude. If not too refined, at all
events too remote, too shadowy and unsubstantial in his modes
of development to suit the taste of the latter class, and yet too
popular to satisfy the spiritual or metaphysical requisition of
the former, he must necessarily find himself without an audience,
except here and there an individual or possibly an isolated
clique. His writings, to do them justice, are not altogether
destitute of fancy and originality; they might have won him
greater reputation but for an inveterate love of allegory which
is apt to invest his plots and characters with the aspect of scenery
and people in the clouds, and to steal away the human warmth
out of his conceptions. His fictions are sometimes historical,
sometimes of the present day, and sometimes, as far as can be
discovered, have little or no reference either to time or space.
In any case, he generally contents himself with a very slight
embroidery of outward manners — the faintest possible counter-
feit of real life — and endeavours to create an interest by some
less obvious peculiarity of the subject. Occasionally, a breath
of Nature, a raindrop of pathos and tenderness, or a gleam of
humor, will find its way into the midst of his fantastic imagery,
and make us feel as if, after all, we were yet within the limits
of our native earth. We will only add to this very cursory

notice that M. de l'Aubépine's productions, if the reader chance
to take them in precisely the proper point of view, may amuse
a leisure hour as well as those of a brighter man; if otherwise,
they can hardly fail to look excessively like nonsense."

This subtle portrait of an author is to be found in the collection of short stories by Nathaniel Hawthorne entitled *Mosses
from an Old Manse*. It forms some sort of preface to the story
called *Rappacini's Daughter*, to which we shall repeatedly return below. The purport is clear, even without the key given
in the name — a name which altogether seems to have been
a prolific source of puns in the style of the age, of which Longfellow's "November nature with a name of May" is one of the
best. We have before us a picture of Nathaniel Hawthorne
such as he saw himself. It must be confessed that his view of
his own character as a writer is creditably free from illusions,
and may still be accepted. Hawthorne has never been very
popular in Europe, and in America he seems chiefly to have
held his position as an interpreter of classical and historical tales
for the young, even if *The Scarlet Letter* always kept an honoured place on the bookshelves for American classics. But, recently, there are signs pointing to a revival of his work on
both sides of the Atlantic. As an example we may mention a
leading article in the *Times' Literary Supplement* of 1928:[1]
"That particular kind of intensity (speaking of *The Scarlet Letter*)
was then rare enough, but manifest in two novels published
from a Yorkshire parsonage in 1847 ... It is perhaps a pre-
judiced opinion to make Emily and Charlotte Brontë the main
determinants of the course of fiction in the 19th century ...
It is perhaps more difficult to see Hawthorne in the modern
American novel — but where is the modern American novel?
It is said to be in the future ... and when it comes, we may
be sure that Hawthorne will be its touchstone."

Although this prophecy may seem rather an audacious one,
there *are* several connecting threads between Hawthorne and
recent American literature. That an interest for these things
exists in America is proved by an article in the New York

[1] *The Times' Literary Supplement*, May 3rd, 1928. Review of *The
Rebellious Puritan* (Nathaniel Hawthorne) by Lloyd Morris. Unsigned.

Times Book Review[1] treating of two recent books on Hawthorne. One of the authors mentioned has, according to the article, "once and for all removed Hawthorne from the Ivory Tower to which critics have long consigned him" and sees him as "a man of wide humanitarian vision who in his own life suffered the temptations of ordinary men," who had "dedicated himself to a creed whose aim was ... a reality to be sought by the individual outside the realm of the material and tangible." The second author reviewed gives "a keen analysis of structure, design, rhythm and tune in Hawthorne's writings" by applying "the principles of painting, sculpture, architecture and music." These works stress Hawthorne's importance to later times. In this essay, my subject is the influence that a particular earlier period can be shown to have exerted on Hawthorne's literary development.[2]

If the external outlines of Nathaniel Hawthorne's life seem to be plain enough, his interior development is more difficult to define. In most biographies and essays written about him, he is termed a Puritan; in many he is also called a Romantic (Romanticist). In order closer to define the subject of this essay, *viz.* Hawthorne's relation to the branch of Romantic literature which has been called the Gothic Romance — later, the "novel of terror and wonder," in France *le roman noir* — I shall attempt to indicate Hawthorne's attitude towards the Puritan inheritance, Romanticism, and his own art.

Puritanism is a term which, to use the words of an American literary critic,[3] is often employed on account of its very haziness. From an historical point of view, the term "puritan" is often used to cover very heterogeneous things. The term may also be employed in its original sense: a zealot for purity. Puritan in this latter sense of the word were men like Milton and Cromwell, but also Emerson, who levelled his criticism against re-

---

[1] *New York Times Book Review*, June 25th, 1944: Two studies of Hawthorne. By Nora Balakian. 1. *Hawthorne, Critic of Society*, by Lawrence Sargent Hall. New Haven, Yale University Press. 2. *Hawthorne, the Artist*. By Leland Schubert, North Carolina University Press.

[2] The present essay is only part of a larger investigation into Hawthorne's work which I am now conducting in the U.S.A.

[3] Kenneth B. Murdock, *The Puritan Tradition in American Literature*. (In *The Reinterpretation of American Literature*).

ligious views and conditions just as well as against ethical or
literary ones. It may be said of American Romanticism — and
especially of the particular form of it that has been called
Transcendentalism — that its foundation was considerably Puritan
in this sense of the word; and, from an historical point of view,
this Puritanism must of course ultimately be derived from Calvinism. Hawthorne, who was in many ways congenial to the
Transcendentalists, had also acquired, by tradition and by education, a close knowledge of the turn of mind inherited by his
countrymen from the first immigrants to New England, and, willy-
nilly, it became an important motive power in his work. We
might here quote one of his recent biographers,[1] who expresses
his view thus: "Hawthorne had been unsparing in his criticism
of Puritan America, but he had been its child . . . In Hawthorne's life . . . the Puritan tradition of his ancestors had been
an active force. He had sought to liberate himself from his
origins and his environment, but they and not he had determined
the character of that effort for emancipation. In Hawthorne,
the Puritan had become an artist." A good specimen of the
view which early literary criticism formed of Hawthorne's
spiritual inheritance from Puritanism was given in 1852 by Émile
Montégut in a review of The Blithedale Romance:[2] ". . . il n'a
plus leur âme (des ancêtres) mais il a leur esprit: il a leur ferme
méthode de stricte investigation et d'impitoyable analyse. Un
descendant des puritains seul pouvait être capable de se livrer
à ce perpétuel examen de conscience que nous trouvons dans
les écrits de M. Hawthorne, à cette confession silencieuse et
muette des erreurs de l'esprit: lui seul était capable d'entre-
prendre ces fouillis dans l'âme humaine pour y découvrir non
des trésors mais des sujets d'épouvante, des reptiles engourdis,
des témoignages de crimes oubliés . . ." To my mind, the de-
finition of Hawthorne's relation to the Puritan inheritance given
by the Swedish essayist Klara Johansson and, as she states,
first formed by John Macy, penetrates to the core of the matter
when she says that[3] "Hawthorne is a Puritan heir only collater-

[1] Lloyd Morris, The Rebellious Puritan. London, 1928.
[2] La revue des deux mondes, 1st Dec., 1852.
[3] Klara Johansson, Det speglade livet. Stockholm, 1924.

ally with his artistic exertions which are intrinsically heathen"
and that the Puritan strain in him is far from the most important feature of his work. Hawthorne is always first and foremost an artist, and the conscience problems of the Puritans are
to him only means which he employs in order to attain an
artistic effect. As a parallel to Hawthorne's self-characterization
cited above ("Occasionally , . . a gleam of humor will find its
way into the midst of his fantastic imagery, and make us feel
as if, after all, we were yet within the limits of our native
earth"), I should like to quote these words of Klara Johansson's:
"*The Scarlet Letter* is no doomsday tale of guilt and repent-
ance, but an exquisite and wholly successful experiment in black
and red. From an ethical point of view, it cannot stand a
scrutiny, but the author uses a special trick of his, continually
to avert such a scrutiny, by his perfect artistry. An irony, as
slight as a momentary luminous reflection in running water,
gleams here and there, as if to suggest that the author does
not take his ethical problem more seriously than it merits to
be taken." We shall find the psychological explanation of this
turn of mind in the deep scepticism which was an essential
feature of Hawthorne's character. The same scepticism was also
to tinge his reaction towards the literary movement that cha-
racterizes his epoch, i. e. Romanticism.

*   *   *

The intellectual and literary life of America at this time
centred in New England — especially in Boston — and was
in a state of seething activity. The rebellion against the philosophical, social and literary ideals of the eighteenth century
which, coming from Europe, reached America between 1820
and 1850 underwent a change in its new environment and appeared in a partly different character. America impressed its
stamp on the new ideas, a stamp which was partly coloured
by the strain of Calvinism in its traditions. The thought of
Kant and Fichte became known directly in the U. S. A — though
more often indirectly through Schelling, as interpreted by Cole-
ridge and Wordsworth. The foremost representative of the American Romantic school, generally called Transcendentalism, was

Emerson who, both theoretically and practically, transposed, in an original manner, the new cravings for self-culture, sincerity and independence, suffusing them with a poetically pantheistic religiosity. But Emerson and his circle adopted only part of the ideology of the European Romantic Movement. There was a distinction, as H. Mumford Jones observes,[1] between foreign orthodoxy and foreign heterodoxy: "Thus it is that the normal idealism of the Romantic movement came in, and the moral anarchy of that movement was kept out, so that we have no American Shelley, no Godwin, no Gautier, no Heine, and no Schopenhauer to deny the conventional values, but in place of these, Emerson and Longfellow and Bryant and Hawthorne, who have their merits doutbless, but who are not quite of the company of Nietzsche." Romanticism advanced in two main currents, one coming from England, and the other from Germany, though there were of course also others; French literature was well-known to the Boston literary public. Acquaintance with the novels, short stories, and poetry of the new authors further encouraged readers to take note of the articles in the British periodicals, which were now enjoying their full lustre in England and Scotland, and soon found equivalents in American political and literary magazines and reviews. While thus the Lakists and prose-writers such as Godwin, Carlyle, and Dickens, and their British contemporaries, were read in original, acquaintance with Hoffmann, Tieck, Fouqué, and other continental authors was often effected through translations or descriptive articles in the periodicals. The literary atmosphere was loaded with Romantic influences; there stood, to use the words of H. M. Belden in his penetrating analysis of Poe's criticism of Hawthorne,[2] "an aura of second and third hand knowledge around every star in the literary firmament."

We know that Hawthorne's knowledge of German was pretty shallow, even after his marriage to Sophia Peabody, who was very well versed in foreign languages. The fact is asserted in

---

[1] H. Mumford Jones, *The European Background*. In *The Reinterpretation of American Literature*.
[2] Henry Marvin Belden, *Poe's Criticism of Hawthorne*. Anglia, XXIII, 1900.

her journal,[1] and also by some items in his American note-books.[2] His reactions to the German Romantic movement have been objects of close investigation by a number of scholars;[3] their main results are summed up in the following quotation from Wilhelm Veen's study of Hawthorne's technique: ". . . wird man somit der Wahrheit wohl am nächsten kommen mit der Annahme, dass Hawthorne deutsche Werke und insbesondere Tiecks wohl gekannt aber sehr wenig geschätzt hat, und dass daher, ganz abgesehen von dem Fehlen auch sichtbarer Spuren von einem Einfluss Tiecks auf Hawthorne schon aus diesen Gründen keine Rede sein kann." On the other hand, the same author stresses the strong influence experienced by Hawthorne from English, American and French literary currents of the time: "In weitaus überwiegender Menge sind es Engländer, von denen einige Namen auch noch beharrlich wiederkehren. Dann kommen gleich die Amerikaner und nach ihnen die Franzosen." In consequence, it seems to be chiefly in English literature that the influences received by Hawthorne from the novel of terror and wonder ought to be traced.

*   *   *

On English soil, prose fiction had, already during the last decades of the eighteenth century, developed two forms, the novel and the romance, which were defined by the novelist

---

[1] *Sophia Peabody's Journal*, July—September, 1838: "Mary invited him to come with his sister on Saturday and read German; but it seems to me he does not want to go on with German." Quoted from J. Hawthorne, *Hawthorne and his Wife*. Boston, 1894.

[2] *The American Note-books*, 1843, April 8th: "After journalizing yesterday afternoon, I went out and sawed and split wood till teatime, then studied German (translating "Lenore") with an occasional glance at a beautiful sunset . . . After lamplight finished "Lenore" . . ."

[3] E. A. Poe, *Hawthorne's Tales*.

E. D. Forgues, *Nathaniel Hawthorne, La revue des deux mondes*, 15.4. 1852.

A. Schönbach, *Beiträge zur Charakteristik Nathaniel Hawthornes*, *Anglia*, 1886.

H. M. Belden, *Poe's Criticism of Hawthorne, Anglia*, 1900.

Walter Just, *Die romantische Bewegung in der amerikanischen Literatur: Brown, Poe, Hawthorne*. Weimar, 1910.

Wilhelm Veen, *Die Erzählungstechnik in den Kurzerzählungen Nathaniel Hawthornes*. Münster, 1939.

Clara Reeve in the following manner:[1] "The Novel is a picture
of real life and manners. and of the times in which it is written.
The Romance, in lofty and elevated language, describes what
never happened nor is likely to happen." The latter of these
groups has been divided by modern scholars[2] into three sec-
tions: the historical, the Gothic, and the Oriental romance. The
first exponent of the first class would be Leland's *Longsword*;
the other two are respectively introduced by Horace Walpole's
Castle of Otranto and William Beckford's *Vathek*. Often, the
three groups merge into one — elements of Gothic romance
are profusely found in *Vathek* and likewise in the historical
romance — for examples we refer to its consummate master,
Sir Walter Scott. The development of Gothic romance in England and on the Continent has attracted many investigators,
among whom we refer to Helene Richter and Alice M. Killen.[3]
The latter scholar counts among the pioneers of the Gothic
school not only Horace Walpole but also Clara Reeve, author
of a series of thrillers very popular in her day, among which
The Old English Baron is to-day the best known. As masters
of the craft Miss Killen designates Ann Radcliffe, a prolific writer
of nerve-racking and mysterious stories, among which we mention *The Italian* and *The Mysteries of Udolpho*, and Matthew
Gregory Lewis, whose unique masterpiece, *The Monk*, marks
the climax of the Gothic craze. As their disciples she names
Beckford, author of the already mentioned Oriental romance
Vathek, and Godwin, who followed an individual trend with
his humanitarian novels of adventure, of which *Caleb Williams*
is the best known. In this category she also classes the Rev.
Mathurin, author of *Melmoth*, who was, however, certainly regarded by his contemporaries as ranking quite as high as the
so-called masters of the school.

In Germany, the Gothic novel was cherished by the Romanticists, who in the beginning of the 19th century continued

---

[1] Cited from Wilbur L. Cross, *The Development of the English Novel*,
London 1905. Cp. p. 30 of the present essay.

[2] Wilbur L. Cross, *The Development of the English Novel*, London,
1905.

[3] Helene Richter, *Geschichte der englischen Romantik*. Halle, 1911.
Alice M. Killen, *Le roman terrifiant ou roman noir de Walpole à
Anne Radcliffe*. Paris, 1924.

on the path paved by the English authors. *Die Elixiere des Teufels* by E. T. A. Hoffmann shows nearly all of the traditional features of Gothic romance, though they have here been lifted to an artistically higher level than ever before. It was not long before the German authors found out that themes of this kind were better suited for shorter treatment, and it is on German soil that the short story of terror first appears. Apart from Hoffmann, it was cultivated also by Tieck, Fouqué, Spiess, and others among the German romanticists. In French literature, features of Gothic romance are to be found in George Sand, in Nodier, and Balzac — especially in the juvenile productions of the latter.[1]

The literary communications between England and the New World were good and astonishingly rapid already during the eighteenth century. *Pamela* was printed in America in 1744 (in England in 1740), *Rasselas* in 1768 (in England in 1759), and *The Vicar of Wakefield* in 1772 (in England in 1768). I have not been able to find exact printing dates for the works of the Gothic school, but it may safely be assumed that they were widely read by the American public. In America, the style was cultivated by Charles Brockden Brown (d. 1810) whose works, according to contemporary testimony,[2] had "the merit of calling for the passions and engaging the sympathy of the reader by means hitherto unemployed by preceding authors." The critic proceeds: "Puerile superstition and exploded manners, Gothic castles and chimeras, are the materials usually employed for this use." Brockden Brown is usually considered as a follower of Godwin. "All his four novels," writes John Erskine,[3] "*Wieland, The Man of Honor, Arthur Mervyn* and *Ormond*, wear the colours of *Caleb Williams*."

As has already been said, German literature reached America chiefly via the periodicals. Carlyle's interpretations of "German Romance," which were printed in England in 1827, appeared in an American edition in 1841. Starting in 1852, the *Demo-*

---

[1] It is known that Hawthorne was sufficiently familiar with Balzac's works.
[2] *Edgar Huntley*, in 1799, cited in van Doren, *The American Novel*.
[3] In the *Cambridge History of American Literature*.

cratic Review published, for a period of six years, one or more
short stories or poems translated from the German in nearly
every issue. Before 1843, at least a dozen of Tieck's short
stories had been translated and printed in America. The short
story of terror and wonder cherished by the Germans was im-
ported into America about 1820 by Washington Irving. His
Tales of a Traveller are, however, characterized by a rather
generous admixture of Anglo-Saxon humour and common sense.
The weird atmosphere is skilfully caught, but the mysteries
generally find a rational if not prosaic explanation at the end
of the story. The unequalled master of the story of terror in
America, and perhaps also in Europe, was later on E. A. Poe,
who has been called "a born Goth."

*   *   *

Horace Walpole's Italian castle, this "croquant féodale" as
it has been called by a French critic[1] a century after its creation, cannot boast of any structural beauty of a classical kind,
and as little of any artistic elevation or historical truth. And
yet it remains a literary monument of high importance that reflects itself even in the novels of today. The mysteriousness,
the ghostly atmosphere, appeal to kindred depths in the human
soul, and there are few authors belonging to the generation that
grew up during the golden age of the Gothic novel, who have
escaped being consciously or subconsciously impressed by its
potent if somewhat ridiculous pathos. When I now proceed to
investigate its influence on Nathaniel Hawthorne, I shall first
try shortly to characterize the principal traits of the novel of
terror and wonder.[2]

---

[1] Charles de Rémusat, *Horace Walpole. Revue des deux mondes,* 15.4.
1852.
[2] My statements are partly based on the researches of A. M. Killen
and Helene Richter mentioned above, and further on the lecture on the
American novel of terror, delivered by Professor S. B. Liljegren at Upsala,
on October 12th, 1944. All these authorities have found it convenient to
classify the principal attributes of these novels in a sort of table; when I
now use the same method, I do so with a view to securing a surveyable
basis for my analysis.

1. The Manuscript.

The authors of the novels of terror and wonder have a great predilection for the trick of telling a story at second hand. One of the characters of an introductory story gives an account of his experiences, or, better still, produces an old manuscript, where the happenings are written down. By supposing parts of the manuscript to be unreadable, the author may evade difficult or unexplicable passages in his tale, as is the case in Mathurin's *Melmoth*; he may even pass off the whole of his work as a translation of an old document, as Walpole did when he first brought out *The Castle of Otranto*.

2. The Castle.

The Gothic castle of Walpole forms the gloomy background of most Gothic novels. It contains numerous secret cabinets and corridors and a labyrinthine network of subterranean passages. Sometimes it is transformed into a convent or the abode of an alchemist or of an erudite inventor of some miraculous or fatal elixir. The castle and its effect on the beholder may be illustrated by an example from *The Mysteries of Udolpho*:

"Another gate delivered them into the second court, grass-grown, and more wild than the first, where, as she surveyed through the twilight its desolation, its lofty walls, overtopt with briony, moss and nightshade, and the embattled towers that rose above — long suffering and murder came to her thoughts . . . The sentiment was not diminished when she entered an extensive Gothic hall, obscured by the gloom of evening."

3. The Crime.

The principal theme consists of a mysterious crime, not infrequently illicit or incestuous love, and at times perpetrated by a person in holy orders. Of all the sin-laden culprits who people the world of the Gothic novel, the Abbot of Matthew Gregory Lewis is the most incumbered. Of him it is said that he was finally accused "not only of rape and murder: the crime of sorcery was laid to his charge."

2—46535

4. Religion.

One or several of the dramatis personae are often monks or have some kind of tie with religion. Lewis's abbot may also here serve as an example. The Inquisition plays a prominent part. The phenomenon of stigmatization which not infrequently occurs, also has affinities in religion.

5. Italians.

The villain of the piece is generally an Italian. This device follows an old tradition, going back to the influence of the Catholic excommunication of Macchiavelli.[1] Sometimes a Spaniard may be substituted for the Italian. Italians are e. g. Schedoni in Radcliffe's *The Italian,* and Montoni in *The Mysteries of Udolpho* by the same author. Spaniards are Lewis's monk, Ambrosio, and Monçada in *Melmoth.* The villains have often pledged themselves to the devil. They are tempted by him and are finally fetched by him. Such is the case in *Vathek,* where Carathis ends her life in the subterranean domains of the giaour, where "her heart becomes a receptacle of eternal fires and she continues to revolve without intermission," and in *The Monk,* where the scene expands into one of the most effective and terrifying canvasses ever painted by a Gothic master:

"The devil: . . . Villain, resign your hopes of pardon. Thus, I secure my prey.

"As he said this, darting his talons into the monk's shaved crown, he sprang with him from the rock. The caves and mountains rang with Ambrosio's shrieks. The demon continued to soar aloft, till reaching a dreadful height, he released the sufferer. Headlong fell the monk through the airy waste; the sharp point of a rock received him; and he rolled from precipice to precipice, till bruised and mangled, he rested on the river's banks. Life still existed in his miserable frame; he attempted in vain to raise himself; his broken and dislocated limbs refused to perform their office, nor was he able to quit the spot where he had first fallen . . . Blind, maimed, helpless and despairing,

---

[1] Cp. the Macchiavelli figure in Marlowe's *Jew of Malta* and Richardson's declaration that he classed his figures as "men, women, or Italians." Cp. also Mario Praz' essay on Machiavelli in English literature.

venting his rage in blasphemy and curses, execrating his existence, yet dreading the arrival of death destined to yield him
up to greater torments, six miserable days did the villain lan-
guish. On the seventh a violent storm arose: the winds in fury
rent up rocks and forests; the sky was now black with clouds,
now sheeted with fire; the rain fell in torrents; it swelled the
stream; the waves overflowed their banks; they reached the spot
where Ambrosio lay, and when they abated, carried with them
into the river the corpse of the despairing monk."

Melmoth meets a similar fate: ". . . . he fell, and falling
grasped at aught that might save him. His fall seemed perpendicular — there was nought to save him — the rock was
as smooth as ice — the ocean of fire broke at its foot . . . he
fell — he blazed — he shrieked. The burning waves boomed
over his sinking head, and the clock of eternity rung out its
awful chime — Room for the soul of the Wanderer."

6. Deformity.

Another attribute of the villain, which appears a little later,
possibly caused by the Romantic predilection for motives from
folklore, is a deformity of some kind or other. Quasimodo, the
dwarf of Notre Dame in Victor Hugo's novel, is such a figure.

7. Ghosts.

Ghosts abound in the stately chambers and subterranean
passages of the Gothic mansions. They may be real spirits of
a supernatural kind, like the huge helmet in the *Castle of
Otranto,* or the model ghost from Clara Reeve's *Old English
Baron*, which appears to the enemies of the hero when they
one night keep watch in a haunted room: "As they stood with
their fists clenched, on a sudden they were alarmed by a dismal
groan from the room underneath. They stood like statues,
petrified by fear, yet listening with trembling expectation. A
second groan increased their consternation; and soon after a
third completed it. They staggered to a seat, and sank down
upon it ready to faint; presently, all the doors flew open, a
pale glimmering light appeared at the door from the staircase,
and a man in complete armour entered the room; he stood

with one hand extended, pointing to the outward door." They
may also be arrayed in shrouds like the mother of Antonia in
The Monk: ". . . suddenly she (Antonia) fancied that she heard
a low sigh draw near her . . . Gracious God, she said to herself, what could be that sound? Was I deceived, or did I really
hear it? Her reflections were interrupted by a voice at the door
scarcely audible; yet the bolt she knew to be fastened, and
this idea in some degree assured her. Presently the latch was
lifted up softly, and the door moved with caution backwards
and forwards . . . Slowly and gradually the door turned upon
its hinges, and standing upon the threshold she beheld a tall
thin figure, wrapped in a white shroud which covered it from
head to foot . . . The figure pointed to the ground with one
hand, and with the other raised the linen which covered its face.

"Almighty God. My mother."
Antonia shrieked and fell senseless upon the floor."

The apparitions may also be false ghosts, *viz.* phenomena
that seem supernatural to the beholder, but are afterwards
rationally explained. Regularly of such a character are the
ghosts and other mysteries evoked by Mrs. Radcliffe, who takes
pains to explain e. g. certain mysterious blue lights as electrical
phenomena.

To this section belong also the sepulchral and graveyard
mysteries, conveying the sinister and tragic atmosphere so es-
sential to Romantic poetry.

8. Magic.

Witches and sorcerers are often met with in these novels,
perhaps oftener in the Oriental variety and in the later German
short stories of terror and wonder than in the English Gothic
romance. Carathis, the mother of Vathek, is a witch, and gives
the following self-characterization to show the legitimacy of her
claims to the title: ". . . I myself have a great desire to . .
visit the subterranean palace, which no doubt contains whatever
can interest persons like us; there is nothing so pleasing as
retiring to caverns; my taste for dead bodies and everything

like mummy is decided." Enchanted objects, magic potions, amulets, etc., are to be found in great profusion.

9. Nature.

For the purpose of evoking sensations of terror, the authors of these novels frequently avail themselves of natural phenomena, sometimes rather surprisingly stressed to serve the terrifying purpose. A deep darkness often attends the crucial events. Rain is falling, wind is blowing, lightnings are flashing and thunders rolling. The pale glimmer of the moon has quite another function for the Gothic authors than for the elegiac poets: its dim light only enhances the prevailing terror. It is night when Matilda (*The Monk*) leads Ambrosio to the subterranean cavern: "A profound obscurity hovered through the void; damp vapours struck cold the friar's heart, and he listened sadly to the blast while it howled along the lonely vaults." When Lucifer appears, we find that "the lightning flashed around him, and the thunder with repeated bursts seemed to announce the dissolution of nature." Cp. also the example from *The Monk* under (5).

Apart from these more or less regular phenomena, prodigies of different kinds also occur. When the Indian magician after having undergone most uncivil treatment has transformed himself into a great ball and rolled away, the irritated Vathek, in exasperation, regards the stars and reproaches them with treachery: "but lo! On a sudden the clear blue sky appeared streaked over with streams of blood, which reached from the valley even to the city of Samarah."

10. Armoured Knights etc.

As has already partly been seen in the example of ghostly appearances in *The Old English Baron* (7), the stage-properties of the Gothic scene include numerous sets of armours, shields, helmets, etc. It is well known that, according to Walpole's own statement, he had got his original inspiration for his novel in a dream of an iron-clad fist, and in *The Castle of Otranto* we find things like the huge helmet which has fallen down from the clouds into the court-yard of the castle and plays a strange and decisive part in the action of the novel. When Manfred shows his intention of pursuing Isabella, once the intended bride of his son, it is said that "the moon, which was now up and gleamed[1] in at the opposite casement, presented to his sight the plumes of the fatal helmet, which rose to the height of the windows, waving backwards and forwards in a tempestuous manner, and accompanied with a hollow and rustling sound."

11. Works of Art.

The mysterious influence of works of art is related to the previous section, and presents themes of endless variability. Portraits endowed with a life of their own that step out of their frames or content themselves with rolling their eyes or uttering some fateful words, belong to the best beloved supernatural appearances of this kind. We remember the walking portrait in *The Castle of Otranto*: "Manfred . . . had advanced some steps after her, still looking backwards on the portrait, when he saw it quit its pannels, and descend on the floor with a grave and melancholy air." In *The Old English Baron*, two portraits of the same lively kind form part of the furniture of the room where the spectres appear, and when the hero in *Melmoth* first catches sight of the fatal family portrait, Mathurin describes the impression he receives by saying that, had he known them, he would have cited Southey's lines from Thalaba:

> "Only the eyes had life,
> They gleamed with demon light."

In Mrs. Radcliffe's *Mysteries of Udolpho* there is also to be found a veiled picture that inspires the poor heroine with indescribable horror. Like all the mysteries of Mrs. Radcliffe's this one, too, is finally given a natural explanation. Even pieces of sculpture may show signs of life. In *The Castle of Otranto*, there is a marble statue that is suddenly seen to bleed.[2] Later on, optical illusions partly supplanted the rôle of the animated works of art.

In this connection the mirrors, which play an important part in many magic tricks and illusions, must also be mentioned.

---

[1] Cp. No. (9).
[2] Cp. p. 23.

Where human eyes are deceived, the looking-glass may show
the truth. It may also possess visionary virtues, like Mathilda's
mirror (*The Monk*), when she tempts Ambrosio by showing him
the picture of Antonia: "She put the mirror into his hand.
Curiosity induced him to take it, and to wish that Antonia
might appear. Matilda pronounced the magic words. Immediately
a thick smoke arose from the characters upon the borders, and
spread itself over the surface. It dispersed again gradually; a
confused mixture of colours and images presented themselves
to the friar's eyes, which at length arranging themselves in their
proper places, he beheld in miniature, Antonia's lovely form."

12. **Blood.**

Quantities of blood ooze through the whole of this literature.
In the subterranean passages, heroes and villains find their way
by tracing more or less mysterious trails of blood. Persons
long deceased show a strong tendency to bleed, preferably
through the nostrils, a phenomenon which every contemporaneous
reader knew to constitute an accusation of murder. Should a
corpse show signs of life, there are also strong reasons for
suspecting a case of suspended animation, caused by some magic
draught. It may also happen that statues begin to bleed, as
mentioned above (11). When Manfred in *The Castle of Otranto,*
in the presence of Alfonso's statue, announces his intention of
divorcing his lawful wife in order to marry Isabella, Walpole
tells us that "As he spoke those words, three drops of blood
fell from the nose of Alfonso's statue ... Behold, said the
friar; mark this miraculous indication that the blood of Alfonso
will never mix with that of Manfred." We also recall the
prodigy in *Vathek*, which consisted of bloody streaks in the sky.[1]

Over the terrifying or wonderful dramas played on the stages
of Gothic romance, with their sinister walls and turrets silhouetted
against backgrounds dyed in a bloody red, chance sways a
pretty omnipotent sceptre. Time or place never constitute any
impediments to the most incredible coincidences and encounters.
However high the difficulties of the heroes and heroines may
pile up, the reader may look forward with almost unerring

[1] Cp. p. 21.

certainty to the final appearance of some *deus ex machina* con-
ferring liberation and rewarding virtue. Neither the composition nor the psychological development of the Gothic novel can
boast of anything very like logic, and humour is altogether unknown to its authors. Its machinery is, as we have found,
rather simple, and the success of each work depends on the
author's resourcefulness and fantasy, his talent for conveying a
weird and ghostly atmosphere, and his flair for nerve-racking
effects. From comparatively unimportant beginnings, as a reaction against the rationalism and formal severity of the eighteenth century, Gothic romance grew into one of the most
powerful currents in the general literature of the nineteenth
century. Without exaggeration, the assertion may be made that
no form of novel-writing has ever been as productive as the
novel of terror and wonder. I shall now proceed to investigate
how, and to what an extent, it may have influenced Nathaniel
Hawthorne.

                    *   *   *

    The student of Hawthorne's life and writings is usually re-
garded as a privileged person because of the fact that Hawthorne's posthumous note-books, manuscripts, and letters have
been so scrupulously kept and published. It is true that his
widow, out of misguided zeal and exaggerated modesty, made
a great many deletions and alterations in his manuscripts before
she authorized their publication, in order to weed out items and
remarks concerning the family or herself that she deemed im-
proper. But on the whole, all this extensive material remains
intact. Day by day, the reader may follow Hawthorne's life,
step by step the composition of his romances and stories. As
has already been remarked, Hawthorne applied the method of
the later naturalistic school: he made notes of every spectacle,
every acquaintance, idea or memory that might be turned to
literary use. But there are nearly no notes on his reading.
The scholar who is looking for literary influences on Hawthorne
must therefore avail himself largely of the method of indirect
induction. During my work on this essay, I have had direct
access only to printed editions of Hawthorne's note-books and

his unfinished manuscripts. The letters have not been available to me otherwise than as quotations in the works of various other authors.

It has been pointed out that the chief Gothic novels written in English may be presumed to have been well known in America during the first decades of the nineteenth century, while the works of the German writers were only partly translated or reviewed in the periodical press. Hawthorne's own disposition, and the environment in which he grew up, made him receptive, from the beginning, towards tales concerning the supernatural world. In the above-mentioned review of Morris's biography,[1] we find an excellent characterization of Hawthorne's attitude: ". . . he was no mystic, and was, if anything, repelled by mysticism. But he was absorbed in something which is often confused with mysticism — in mystery and mysteriousness. And this fact is really the clue to his character, if we can arrive at an understanding of it." In the introduction to his edition of Hawthorne's first diary, Samuel T. Pickard mentions a letter from one of the young Nathaniel's friends, W. Symmes, who wrote in later years:[2] "One of your correspondents . . . describes the mother of Nathaniel as being somewhat superstitious, and from what I recollect of her, he is correct. Not a gross and ignorant, but a polished and pious superstition. Perhaps this proclivity in the parent may account for his filling his journal with so many of the local stories of the supernatural." The stories referred to treat of Pulpit Rock Hill, from which the devil was said to have preached to the Indians, thereafter to make them sink down into a swamp, so that great masses of skeletons were still lying under the surface of the field — or of an enchanted apple-tree, whose fruit was guarded by spirits, so that the reapers were in constant danger of being hit by stones thrown from nowhere — or of a bewitched house, the windows of which perpetually sprang open, etc., etc. Certainly Nathaniel also heard in childhood many of the stories from the early immigration days when witchery was rampant among the

---

[1] *The Times Literary Supplement*, May 3rd, 1928.
[2] *Hawthorne's First Diary*. With an Account of its Discovery and Loss, by Samuel T. Pickard. London 1897.

pious settlers — stories which have left so many traces in his later works.

Like any other American schoolboy, Hawthorne was, from his early youth, acquainted with the English classics. Spenser and Bunyan are generally indicated as the most important sources of inspiration derived from his early reading. Randall Stewart[1] also mentions Shakespeare and Milton. A. Turner, in his treatise on Hawthorne's literary borrowings,[2] points to the important influence wrought on Hawthorne by the historical writings of Increase and Cotton Mather on the legends and customs of 17th century Massachusetts, especially stressing "the Mather witch tradition" with its accounts of witch meetings, ridings through the air on broomsticks, etc., which we shall meet in some of Hawthorne's stories, e. g. "Young Goodman Brown."[3] As to the literature of terror and wonder, we have direct evidence of his having read some of the best-known novels in a couple of letters written to his sister Elizabeth. On September 28th, 1819, he writes:[4] "I have read Waverley, Roderick Random and the first volume of The Arabian Nights." And on October 31st, 1820:[5] "I have read Hogg's Tales, Caleb Williams, St. Leon and Mandeville. I admire Godwin's Novels, and intend to read them all." The deep impression which Mathurin's *Melmoth* had made on him is apparent in the evident traces that its reading has left on his first novel, *Fanshawe,* as also in the fact that the motto of one of its chapters is directly drawn from *Melmoth.* An item in his English note-book of 1857 shows that Walpole's *The Castle of Otranto* was once familiar to him. Hawthorne is wandering about in a picture-gallery, and remarks:[6] "Of all the older pictures, the only one that I took pleasure in looking at, was a portrait of Lord Deputy Falkland, by Van-

---

[1] Randall Stewart, *The American Note-books.* New York 1932. — The author classifies Hawthorne's villains into three types, of which one, the type of Chillingworth, "old men stooped and gray," traces his ancestry to Spenser's Archimago (*Faerie Queene* I. 1.29. 1—7). He also refers to Milton's *Paradise Lost* IV, 127—130.
[2] A. Turner, *Hawthorne's Literary Borrowings. Publications of the Modern Language Association of America,* 1936.
[3] Cp. pages 35, 36, 37 of the present essay.
[4] Cited from J. Hawthorne, *Nathaniel Hawthorne and his Wife.*
[5] Cited from Randall Stewart, *Hawthorne's American Note-books.*
[6] *Hawthorne's English Note-book,* July 30th, 1857.

somer, in James I's time — a very stately, full-length figure in white, looking out of the picture as if he saw you. The catalogue says that this portrait suggested an incident in Horace Walpole's Castle of Otranto; but I do not remember it."

That the contemporaries of Hawthorne, or at least his European critics, were fully aware of the fact that a considerable part of his literary background was of the traditional Gothic kind, is clearly shown by an article in the *Revue des deux mondes*, of 1852,[1] by E. D. Forgues. The writer is speaking of the rôle assigned to the portrait of Colonel Pyncheon in *The House of the Seven Gables*: "Ce portrait se trouve mêlé à l'action, où il joue le rôle réservé aux fantômes avant l'invention de la peinture à l'huile: c'est lui qui cache le document perdu; c'est lui qui suspend et dénoue la chaîne des revenants, comme Walter Scott, Lewis, Mme Radcliffe et Washington Irving, sans parler de Maturin, de Hoffmann et de bien d'autres encore, en ont tous écrit."

Hoffmann is here mentioned in the same breath as the English and American authors of novels of terror and wonder. We have already discussed the question of Hawthorne's acquaintance with the German Romanticists, and only a few facts shall here be added. Contemporary criticism sometimes accused Hawthorne of being influenced by the Germans. As an example may be cited an article in the *National Magazine* of 1853[2] where it is cursorily remarked: "Saving certain shadowy resemblances to some of the Germans..." and above all Poe's criticism of *Mosses from an Old Manse*, where he deliberately accuses Hawthorne of having imitated Tieck. The critical discussion of this problem has attracted many participants (Cp. p. 13, note 3) but may be regarded as settled. H. M. Belden[3] has succeeded in proving beyond doubt that Hawthorne may have read in translation some of Tieck's better-known tales before 1833, but that the imitation with which Poe tried to charge him is exceedingly unlikely. Another scholar who has thoroughly examined

---

[1] E. D. Forgues, *Nathaniel Hawthorne. La revue des deux mondes.* 15.4. 1852.
[2] Cited from Bertha Faust, *Hawthorne's Contemporaneous Reputation.* Philadelphia, 1939.
[3] *Anglia*, 1900.

the possibilities of European influence on Hawthorne's writings,
A. Schönbach, arrives at a similar result:[1] "Am ehesten räume
ich noch Balzac etwas Einfluss auf Hawthorne ein, ferner mag
sein Liebling Walter Scott ihn ermutigt haben, die Geschichten
aus der Colonialzeit zu schreiben, später hat er noch von Dickens
ein weniges gewonnen. Aber, wie Poe glaubte, und seither mit
Ausdauer nachgeschrieben wird, dass Tieck Hawthornes Muster
gewesen und von ihm nachgebildet worden sei, das ist mir schon
aus diesen inneren Gründen höchst unwahrscheinlich. In Tiecks
Erzählungen sind Dargestelltes und Darsteller von derselben
Stimmung erfüllt: wird das Reale an einer Stelle verlassen, dann
aber sofort auch an allen und im Ganzen." To Hawthorne's
attitude towards the unreal and supernatural we will revert later
on. First, we shall for a moment occupy ourselves with the
possibilities of an influence from the earlier American versions
of the Gothic novel.

The most prominent representative of the Gothic school
in America was, as has already been said, Charles Brockden
Brown. It is to be assumed that Hawthorne was well versed
in his tales. An American scholar, Professor Quinn, who has
devoted a study[2] to the rôle of the supernatural in the literature
of his country, is of opinion that no impressions of real import
derive from this source: "Brown, however, has little direct influence upon Poe or Hawthorne." We have greater reason to
assume an influence from Washington Irving. From the point
of view of literary form, it is likely that Hawthorne acquired
something of his early predilection for the short story by reading
the works of his countryman. There are also stylistic similarities.
Woodberry remarks:[3] "From the former (the eighteenth century)
he had that pellucid style, whose American flow began with
Washington Irving and ceased with his own pen." But neither
in respect of actual plots, nor when it comes to the general
trend of ideas, need we believe Hawthorne to be indebted to
the author of the *Tales of a Traveller* — so perfect in their

---

[1] *Anglia,* 1886.
[2] Quinn, *Some Phases of the Supernatural in American Literature.
Modern Language Association of America,* XVIII, Baltimore, 1910.
[3] Woodberry, *Hawthorne, How to Know Him.*

kind, where common sense pervades the atmosphere far too thoroughly to permit any kind of transcendental extravagance.

There is a close affinity between Hawthorne's taste for magic and supernatural stories and his interest for Swedenborg, for spiritualism and mesmerism, which we find expressed in different ways in his writings and is surreptitiously mentioned in his note-books. During his stay in England, in 1857, he discusses spiritualism thoroughly with some friends, and sums up his own position in a passage in his note-book, which gives a fair idea of his view on these matters:[1] "Do I believe in these wonders? Of course; for how is it possible to doubt either the solemn word or the sober observation of a learned and sensible man like Dr —? But again do I really believe it? Of course not; for I cannot consent to have heaven and earth, this world and the next, beaten up together like the white and yolk of an egg, merely out of respect to Dr —'s sanity or integrity. I would not believe my own sight, nor touch of the spiritual hands; and it would take deeper and higher strains than those of Mr. Harris to convince me. I think I might yield to higher poetry or heavenlier wisdom than mortals in the flesh have ever sung or uttered. Meanwhile, this matter of spiritualism is surely the strangest that ever was heard of, and yet I feel unaccountably little interest in it — a sluggish disgust, and repugnance to meddle with it — insomuch that I hardly feel as if it were worth this page or two in my not very eventful journal." But regarded as literary themes, these things possessed for him an interest as great as all other problems concerning the human soul.

The scenery and the whole machinery of Gothic Romance became, just like Puritanism or Spiritualism, one of Hawthorne's media of artistic expression. He called all his whole-length stories romances,[2] and has given reason for this in the introduction to *The House of the Seven Gables:* "When a writer calls his work a Romance, it need hardly be observed that he wishes to claim a certain latitude, both as to its fashion and material, which he would not have felt himself entitled to assume had

---

[1] *Hawthorne's English Note-book.* December 20th, 1857.
[2] Cp. p. 14.

he professed to be writing a Novel. The latter form of composition is presumed to aim at a very minute fidelity, not merely to the possible, but to the probable and ordinary course of man's experience. The former — while, as a work of art, it must rigidly subject itself to laws, and while it sins unpardonably so far as it may swerve aside from the truth of the human heart — has fairly a right to present that truth under circumstances, to a great extent, of the writer's own choosing or creation. If he think fit, also, he may so manage his atmospherical medium as to bring out or mellow the lights and deepen and enrich the shadows of the picture. He will be wise, no doubt, to make a very moderate use of the privileges here stated, and especially to mingle the Marvellous rather as a slight, delicate, and evanescent flavour, than as any portion of the actual substance of the dish offered to the public. He can hardly be said, however, to commit a literary crime, even if he disregard this caution."

Hawthorne's literary ideal has been in a certain measure foreshadowed by Leigh Hunt who once wrote:[1] "A ghost story, to be a good one, should unite as much as possible objects such as they are in life with a preternatural spirit. And to be a perfect one — at least to add to the other utility of excitement a moral utility." Moral utility is, however, not the accurate term for the aim of Hawthorne's writings. Utility of any kind was hardly sought by this "Artist of the Beautiful."[2] And moralist is certainly not the right word to denote this indefatigable seeker, incessantly hunting for the innermost motives of human actions. Henry James, whose Life of Hawthorne[3] is of a masterly composition but stamped by too much cool insensibility wholly to convince the reader, has, however, in this respect found a good formula: "He was not a moralist," says James, "and he was not simply a poet. The moralists are weightier, denser, richer in a sense; the poets are more purely inconclusive and irresponsible. He combined in a singular degree the spontaneity of the imagination with a haunting care for moral problems."

[1] Cited from Cross, *The Development of the English Novel.* London, 1905.
[2] The title of a story included in *Mosses from an Old Manse.*
[3] Henry James Jr, *Hawthorne.* London, 1902.

It is difficult to find a label to fix on to this methodical and intense, not to say frantic plumber of the depths of sin in the human soul. Childhood remembrances, religious and philosophical conceptions, literary reminiscences, and the creations of his own fantasy are to him only artistic means for throwing a penetrating light over the truths of the human soul, which he believes to have found out during years of never-ceasing, devoted study. His work is of a deeply individual stamp. We cite P. Kaufman who writes:[1] ". . . into traditional form he infused profound brooding and achieved the distinction of making romance profoundly subjective. Hitherto this genre both in prose and verse had been, in the psychological phrase of our day, of extrovert nature. He created an original introvert form true to his own character, thus introducing the recent romantic preoccupation with individual feeling and imagination into the traditional type." But at the same time, Hawthorne always remained the "detached observer" of which Erskine[2] speaks in his biographical study. His oversensibility and his scepticism alike prevented him from giving way to any kind of self-reflection. He consciously sought to avoid any form of it, as he expressly declares in the introduction to *Mosses from an Old Manse*: "Has the reader gone wandering hand in hand with me, through the inner passages of my being, and have we groped together into all its chambers and examined their treasures or their rubbish? Not so. We have been standing in the greensward, but just within the cavern's mouth, where the common sunshine is free to penetrate and where every footstep is therefore free to come. I have appealed to no sentiment or sensibilities, save such as are diffused among us all. So far as I am a man of really individual attributes, I veil my face; nor am I nor have I ever been, one of those supremely hospitable people, who serve up their own hearts delicately fried, with brain-sauce, as a tit-bit for their beloved public." Hawthorne is no psychologist in the proper meaning of the word. Hardly any of his figures possesses a life of its own. They are all embodiments

---

[1] Paul Kaufman, *The Romantic Movement*. In the *Reinterpretation of American Literature*.
[2] In the *Cambridge History of American Literature*.

of ideas that have been made to borrow features from his Puritan forefathers, from honest citizens of Salem or Concord, from the intellectuals of Brook Farm or from artists and tourists he had chanced to meet in his work or during his travels. Not one of them finds his own path, being driven by that inner necessity which may compel a figure of fiction to develop in a way contrary to the original intentions of its creator. They all move more or less like puppets in skilfully constructed tracks which go to prove the author's ethical theories. Of this art, Hawthorne attained an ever-growing mastery.

* * *

I now pass on the proper theme of my investigation, and shall try to trace the influence of the novel of terror and wonder on Hawthorne's writings. I shall treat 15 of Hawthorne's short stories, his youthful romance *Fanshawe,* his four great romances and the four posthumous manuscripts. According to Quinn,[1] 19 of Hawthorne's 79 short stories deal with supernatural themes, but as has already been mentioned, Hawthorne broached subjects related to spiritism or mesmerism which will not be touched upon here. Thanks to E. Lathrop-Chandler's excellent study[2] of the chronology of Hawthorne's early productions, I have been able to take up the stories according to the order in which they were originally written.

The first pages we possess by Hawthorne — except his first note-books — are the fragments of a story contained in the later revised edition of *Alice Doane's Appeal.* When Hawthorne reverted to the intrigue he had invented at 16 years of age, he gave it a congenial setting, placing himself as a narrator, accompanied by two beautiful ladies on Gallow's Hill, where he produces his manuscript. The story begins with a murder, and is then traced back to the description of how the beautiful and virtuous Alice Doane and her brother Leonard, who is obsessed by a diseased imagination, make the acquaintance of Walter Brome, a young man who has formerly led a

[1] Quinn, *Some Phases of the Supernatural in American Literature.*

[2] Elizabeth Lathrop-Chandler, *A Study of the Sources of the Tales and Romances written by Nathaniel Hawthorne before 1853.* Smith College Studies, 1926. Vol. 7, No. 4.

reckless and ungoverned life in Europe (cp. *Melmoth*). There is
a striking resemblance between Walter, who falls in love with
Alice, and Leonard who hates the stranger and feels a strong
jealousy on behalf of his sister. Leonard murders Walter, and
in the same moment recognizes in him his own brother. Then
follows a fantastic description of a moon-lit winter's night, and
suddenly the reader is led on to a graveyard: ". . . each family
tomb had given up its inhabitants, who, one by one, through
distant years, had been borne to its dark chamber, but now
came forth and stood in a pale group together . . . The whole
miserable multitude, both sinful souls and false spectres of good
men, groaned horribly and gnashed their teeth, as they looked
upward to the calm loveliness of the midnight sky, and beheld
those homes of bliss where they must never dwell. Such was
the apparition, though too shadowy for language to portray;
for here would be the moonbeams on the ice, glittering through
a warrior's breastplate, and there the letters of a tombstone, on
the form that stood before it . . . This company of devils and
condemned souls had come on holiday to revel in the discovery
of a complicated crime."

In the original manuscript, which Hawthorne does not cite
in the printed version, there followed after this an explanation
of how the whole horrible story of the incestuous love between
sister and brother and the fratricide was due to the machina-
tions of a wizard, "a small, grey, withered man, with fiendish
ingenuity in devising evil, and superhuman power to execute it."

In this first literary attempt of Hawthorne's, we find no less
than five of the elements in our scheme represented. There are
two crimes, of which one is of an incestuous nature (2), there
is the scene with the spectres assembled in the graveyard (7),
the wizard (8) who is a dwarf (6), and the typically Romantic
description of a moon-lit night (9). Though the manner of
telling the story in the form of repetition from a manuscript
does not belong to its original version, and the manuscript is
not an old parchment but only some sheets of paper from the
author's own drawer, we may also add point (1) of our list of
Gothic characteristics.

The next work with which we shall have to occupy ourselves is *Fanshawe*, the youthful novel that Hawthorne later on wanted to suppress. It is a story from a college, behind which the contours of Bowdoin may readily be traced. The Rector, whose name is Melmoth (sic!), receives in his home a young girl, Ellen Langton, daughter of one of the friends of his youth. Two students, the death-haunted and melancholy Fanshawe — whom one might be tempted to call a Werther if such a likeness did not prevail between him and the young author himself — and the buoyant Walcott, both fall in love with her. A mysterious fisherman, another edition of the Melmoth figure, who has, during his wandering life, become "irrevocably ruined and irreclaimably depraved," appears and takes advantage of a letter he brings from Ellen's father to get an interview with her. The fisherman, Butler, believes Ellen's father to be dead, but does not tell her this. Instead, he tries to elope with her, assisted by the local innkeeper, who has formerly been his companion in pirate adventures. Ellen is saved from his first attempt to abduct her. Afterwards, Melmoth receives a letter from her father, who has been miraculously saved from an impending shipwreck. Ellen disappears anew and is taken by Butler to a cave on the seashore. Walcott and Fanshawe search for the elopers, and Fanshawe catches sight of them from the top of a rock. Butler tries to climb the cliff in order to wrestle with Fanshawe, but slips and is hurled down into the abyss: "When within a few feet of the summit, the adventurer grasped at a twig too slenderly rooted to sustain his weight. It gave way in his hand and he fell backwards down the precipice. His head struck against the less perpendicular part of the rock, whence the body rolled heavily down to the detached fragment, of which mention has heretofore been made. There was no life left in him. With all the passion of hell alive in his heart, he had met the fate that he intended for Fanshawe." The melancholy Fanshawe lacks the courage to make a serious attempt at conquering Ellen's heart and hand. He dies in his twentieth year, and Ellen, as might be expected, marries the more robust Walcott.

This novel displays a whole set of definitive reminiscences from the reading of *Melmoth*. We find them in the motto of one of the chapters, in the headmaster's name, in the description of the mysterious traveller Butler and his catastrophic end.[1]

Fanshawe was begun in August 1816 and published in December 1827. The short story of *The Hollow of the Three Hills* was commenced as early as 1824, but published for the first time in 1830, and afterwards included in the *Twice-told Tales*. In the shadow of a majestic oak on a mantling pool, at a spot that has been known from time immemorial as the resort of the powers of evil, there meet two women: one is old and withered; the other is young, beautiful, pale, and unhappy. The young one puts her head in the old woman's lap, and the latter murmurs a sort of incantation. By faint sounds arriving to her from an illimitable distance of space and time, the young woman then perceives the things that have happened to the people closest related to her, but severed from her by an evil fate.

In this sketch from the early immigration period, we find as instances of our categories: (8), the witch and her magic power, and (9), the description of the surrounding landscape with its traditional weirdness. In his criticism of the stories, Poe has drawn attention to Hawthorne's original manner of remoulding one of the traditional forms of witchery: "It has been the fashion to describe, in such cases, a mirror in which the images of the absent appear; or a cloud of smoke is made to arise, and thence the figures are gradually unfolded. Mr. Hawthorne has wonderfully heightened the effect by making the ear, in place of the eye, the medium by which the fantasy is conveyed."

Young Goodman Brown (written in 1828—29, included in *Mosses from an Old Manse*) is a fantastic, legend-like tale of 17th century Salem, and one of Hawthorne's most suggestive stories. The whole atmosphere of the period and the scene were extremely familiar to the author — both the village street basking in the clear sunshine of the morning, and the picture

---

[1] I cite the descriptions of men falling into abysses at full length because they give one of the best illustrations I have been able to find of an impression made on him by his reading of novels of terror, which followed Hawthorne from boyhood till late in life.

which a superstition-ridden imagination draws of the witch-sabbath
in the depths of the dense woods.

There is very little action in the story. It describes how,
one morning, the young Goodman Brown takes farewell of his
young wife in order — but for a single time — to make an
excursion into the wood, driven by his curiosity as to the midnight revels that the devil is said to hold there. He soon
chances to meet the personage in question, "a man in grave
and decent attire," owner of a quaint staff that bears the likeness of a great wriggling snake which is declared to be "one
of the rods which its owner had formerly lent to the Egyptian
magi." They advance into the wood, and are by and by over-
taken by different well-known people from the little town. There
are the minister and Deacon Gookin, there is old Goody Cloyse,
the pious teacher of catechism to the small children of the
vicinity; now she vanishes into the air, and it is understood
that, having lost her own broomstick, she is riding on the
mysterious rod of the Devil. In the heart of the wood, the
witch sabbath is celebrated. The Devil mounts a sort of pulpit
— we remember the "Devil's pulpit" of Hawthorne's first diary —
and below him assemble the honest citizens and pious widows
and housewives of the town, its ancient spinsters and fair young
girls, mixed with women of bad reputation and men of dissolute
lives, even criminals. "Bring forth the converts," somebody
cries, and Goodman Brown recognizes his Faith among the
crowd, whose otherwise veiled crimes appear in the shades of
the unhallowed night. They are all baptized in blood in a font
which nature has formed in the rock. Goodman Brown staggers
home to Salem, where the street lies calm and peaceful in the
light of the morning sun, where the morning prayer of the
minister is to be heard through an open window and Goody
Cloyse is catechizing a little girl. Faith greets him, but he
cannot answer her as before. Never will Goodman Brown regain
his joy in living. Was his experience real or only a bad dream?

Here we find, fully developed, Hawthorne's method of creating
parables around his constant theme: the question of the rôle of
sin in human life. The setting he has chosen is the Puritan
environment of his ancestors, with its religious severity and its

wealth of superstition. The gloomy atmosphere that surrounds the wanderers in the dark forest is skilfully evoked: Goodman Brown and his companion hear human voices belonging to invisible people on their way to the witches' sabbath, or they see how the moon is obscured though there is no wind, and infer that some human form must have passed through the air. Goody Cloyse possesses all the traditional attributes of a witch. Somebody has stolen her broomstick, "and that too, when I was all anointed with the juice of smallage, and cinquefoil, and wolf's bane," etc. The Devil, who, by his baptism, makes both men and women "partakers of the mystery of sin, more conscious of the secret guilt of others, both in deed and thought, than they could now be of their own," causes the leaves on a bough which he takes in his hand to shrivel and die. The whole thing is a rather exquisite pastiche in the style of Dürer; Hawthorne has already attained perfect mastery of his means of expression.

When now passing on to scrutinize the story in relation to our scheme, we might of course dwell both on the mention of a mysterious crime and on the religious atmosphere; but these ingredients are not used here in a strictly Gothic sense. They rather form an integrating part of Hawthorne's personal message, though they certainly intensify the gloominess of the story. But our category (8) is strongly represented, as is also (9) in the moonlight and the supernatural lull in the wood. Further, we remark the blood (12) of the font in the rock.

The life and manners of the old 17th century Puritans form the environment of several of Hawthorne's best tales from the late twenties, such as *The Grey Champion* (1828—29) and *The May-pole of Merry Mount* (1828—29). Possessing certain claims of being founded on historical tradition, they are rather to be referred to Hawthorne's historical sketches — *Grandfather's Chair* and *The Tanglewood Tales* — and, though they certainly have a somewhat ghostly atmosphere, they will not be further treated here. We pass on instead to *The Great Carbuncle* (1832—33, *Twice-told Tales*).

The theme of this story is taken from a sphere which otherwise does not belong to Hawthorne's stock-in-trade. The great

advance towards the West, the Frontier, the life of settlers and
Indians, is one of the chief themes on which American literature
is founded, and was of an immense importance to many of
Hawthorne's contemporaries. To Hawthorne himself it was of
less vital consequence. Legends and superstitions based on life
in the Western wilds did not captivate his imagination as in-
tensely as did tales about mysterious happenings in a more
cultured contemporary environment, or dealing with early days
in New England or with mediaeval Europe. Nevertheless, we
find here and there glimpses of Indian romance in Hawthorne's
works; it is often coloured by dark and primitive magic. *The
Great Carbuncle* is derived from the Indian legend of a jewel
of supernatural splendour and beauty that is said to exist in
the virgin forest but has never been seen by human eyes. Hawthorne introduces his readers to a little party of seven persons
who have all departed from their homes in quest of the treasure.
The story is of the semi-allegoric, "Hawthornesque" kind; it
illustrates human striving in different forms. One of the seekers
is a merchant, another is a poet. The eldest of them, who is
only called the Seeker, is clad in the skins of wild animals and
is described as follows: "He was one of those ill-fated mortals,
such as the Indians told of, whom, in their early youth, the
great Carbuncle smote with a peculiar madness, and became
the passionate dream of their existence . . . there went a fable
. . . that for this inordinate lust after the Great Carbuncle he
had been condemned to wander among the mountains till the
end of time." At his side sits a doctor Cacophodel, "who had
willed and dried himself into a mummy by continually stooping
over charcoal furnaces, and inhaling unwholesome fumes during
his researches in chemistry and alchemy. It was told . . . that
he had drained his body of all its richest blood, and wasted
it . . . in an unsuccessful experiment." There is also an English
nobleman "who, when at home, was said to spend much of his
time in the burial vault of his dead progenitors, rummaging among
their mouldy coffins in search of all the earthly pride and
vainglory that was hidden among bones and dust." Lastly, the
author presents Hannah and Matthew, a young, newly-married
couple, who in their natural simplicity seem rather out of place

among all the dreamers in the quaint company. The seekers all tell us legends about the mysterious gem, and of the Indian spirit which is said to keep watch over it.

When morning comes, the pilgrims wander about in different directions in search of the Carbuncle — the merchant intending to sell it at an exorbitant price, the lord aiming to give it a fitting place in his ancestral castle, etc. The young couple only want it for embellishing their humble abode, which they want to make as nice and comfortable as possible for each other. After many hours, Hannah and Matthew find themselves surrounded by a dense mist, through which a faint light is gleaming. The light appears to be the Great Carbuncle, glowing from the brow of a cliff on the other side of a lake. At the base of the cliff, they perceive the dead body of the Seeker with his arms extended towards the goal. Hanna and Matthew catch fright at the sight. To them the blessed sunshine and the quiet moonlight suffice. And so they return to their cottage — without the Great Carbuncle. And the fate of the marvellous gem? "It is affirmed that, from the hour when two mortals had shown themselves so simply wise as to reject a jewel which would have dimmed all earthly things, its splendour waned." But there are also some few who believe that the Great Carbuncle is still blazing as of old.

In this fully developed allegory, Hawthorne has made skilful use of the mysteriousness of Indian folklore, which he has interwoven with ideas and events that are well known to readers of the Gothic novels. The description of the Seeker reminds one of many magicians (8), and also the misshapen scholar at his side apparently derives his origin from the long descent of deformed villains in the same kind of literature (8, 5). The carbuncle itself is a still more brilliant variety of the Carbuncle of Giamschid, which is promised to the beautiful Nourounihar if she forsakes her childish betrothed Gulchenrouz for Vathek. The subtitle of the story, *A Mystery of the White Mountains,* itself shows that Hawthorne was quite consciously appealing to his readers' appreciation of the supernatural when, in this modern parable, he tried to depict the vanity of human strivings.

The Wedding Knell (1835, *Twice-told Tales*) is told as a

true story, but nevertheless it has a strong allegorical purport.
The author tells of a New York wedding in the young days of
his grandmother. Neither of the parties were young any longer,
but they had once in their youth been engaged to each other.
He had spent forty years in solitude and become an eccentric
old bachelor. She had been married twice, first to an aged
gentleman with a fortune and, secondly, to a southerner considerably younger than herself. Though widowed anew, she still
tried to play the part of a young woman, and entered the
church at the head of a bridal party made up of youth and
gaiety. The bridegroom was late, and meanwhile the church-
bells began to sound — but it was not the tinkling of the gay
wedding-bells but the heavy toll of the funeral knell. At the
same moment, a hearse with a train of several coaches ap-
proached, and to the great fright of the bridal party, there entered
through the church door a strange crowd: "A dark procession
paced into the church. First came an old man and woman,
like chief mourners at a funeral attired from head to foot in
the deepest black, all but their pale features and hoary hair."
Thereupon followed a whole train of aged people dressed in
mourning. They formed a circle around the altar, and the
bridegroom appeared in their midst: "A form, that had been
worthily ushered in with all this gloomy pomp, the death knell,
and the funeral. It was the bridegroom in his shroud... Come,
my bride, said those pale lips, the hearse is ready ... Let us
be married, and then to our coffins." The bride is as frightened
as the merry wedding-guests, but the bridegroom makes a
speech and proves that it is he who wears the proper garb for
a wedding like this. The spring-time of life is past, and both
of them must prepare for the grave. The bride concedes that
he is right, and her worldliness disappears. The couple are
united, and the organ's peal of solemn triumph mingles itself
with the tolling of the death-bell.

Once more, Hawthorne has here endowed his moral lesson
with impressive force by mingling the mysteriousness of death
and funeral rites with his story. The contrast between the gay
and youthful bridal party and the sinister funeral procession
produces a very striking effect. That the bridegroom in his

shroud is fairly directly drawn from the sepulchral chambers of the novels of terror and wonder (7) is clear. When, in a hollow voice, he tells his bride: "Then to our coffins," he repeats a late echo of the first modern literary ghost ballad, the *Lenore* of Bürger, which, in a way, constitutes the beginning of literary Romanticism in Germany. Hawthorne tells us in an item in his note-book that he is busy translating this piece of poetry from the German, but as the item is entered in 1843,[1] it may not be surmised with certainty that he knew *Lenore* as early as 1836. Still, it is reasonably plain that the sinister summons can be traced back through unknown intermediaries to the ghostly horseman of Bürger, who, in the stormy night, whispers to his beloved on the pommel of his saddle:

"Graut, Liebchen, auch? Der Mond scheint hell.
Hurra. Die Toten reiten schnell ..."

From 1835 also originates *The Prophetic Pictures* (*Twice-told Tales*). The author declares in an introductory note tha the has got the motive of the story from Dunlap's *History of the Art of Design*. The principal figure is a painter, as is so often the case in the novels of terror and wonder. He has no name in the story, and the only thing that is known of his origin, is that he has been born and educated in Europe — the Continent that had also fostered the painter Francesco, master of the picture of Rosalie in Hoffmann's *Elixiere des Teufels*. He is a master of his art, and even more than that: "... he paints not merely a man's features, but his mind and heart. He catches the secret sentiments and passions, and throws them upon the canvas, like sunshine — or perhaps, in the portraits of dark-souled men, like a gleam of infernal fire." He also possesses knowledge in other fields, partly to be classified as magic: he not only excels in his peculiar art, but possesses vast acquirements in all other branches of learning and science. "He talks Hebrew with Dr. Mather, and gives Lectures in anatomy to Dr. Boylston."

[1] *Hawthorne's American Note-book,* April 8th, 1843. Cp. p. 13 of the present essay. Of course, Hawthorne must at an early date have come across one or more of the numerous English translations of *Lenore* of which Walter Scott's version was widely known.

This European has come to America, where he later on travels
about in order to detect the charm of the New World:" . . . the
stern dignity of Indian chiefs, the dusky loveliness of Indian
girls; the domestic life of wigwams . . . The glow of perilous
moments . . . love, hate, grief, frenzy; in a word, all the worn-
out heart of the old earth had been revealed to him under a
new form." Here we chance upon one of the rare cases of
frontier romance in Hawthorne. But the principal theme of the
story is formed by the two portraits, which this painter paints
of Walter Ludlow and his young wife Elinor. His technique is
a strange one: he paints them both at the same time, adding
strokes alternately in a sort of queer interplay, and, according
to his own words, the two pictures are the best things he has
hitherto made. Here, Hawthorne inserts a brief meditation on
the character of portraits and portrait-painting in general, which
we repeat because of the interest it will acquire in our study
of his later works: "Nothing, in the whole circle of human vani-
ties, takes a stronger hold of the imagination than this affair of
having a portrait painted. Yet why should it be so? The
looking-glass, the polished globe of andirons, the mirror, like
water, and all other reflecting surfaces, continually present us
with portraits, or rather ghosts, of ourselves, which we glance
at, and straightway forget them. But we forget them only because they vanish. It is the idea of duration — of earthly
immortality — that gives such a mysterious interest to our
portraits."

The painter goes away on his great American journey, and
the two portraits are given their places of honour in the new
home of Elinor and Walter. They soon begin to exert a sinister influence, and rumours are whispered about them in the
town. Slowly, the features of the pictures change — and the
observer will find the same alterations in the faces of their
models: ". . . had the picture itself been a mirror, it could not
have thrown back her present aspect with stronger and more
melancholy truth." Finally they are covered with a curtain.
The painter returns, and goes to visit the house and look at
the pictures, and it is said that "he seemed to hear the step
of Destiny approaching behind him, on its progress towards its

victims." The young couple are standing before the pictures, the malignant influence of which now decides their fate. Walter draws a dagger and aims it at Elinor's bosom.

Even if Hawthorne here likewise tries to point a sort of moral — if the result of our actions could be set before us, would we then abstain from the evil ones? — the chief motive of the story is not at all a moral one. It consists in the gradually increasing suspense caused by the inherent magic of the pictures (11), and it has been treated with great skill and beauty. The painter, as has already been mentioned, is a figure often found in the works of romantic novelists. The magic of pictures is a popular theme. It was one of the subjects most often treated by Washington Irving (*The Adventure of My Aunt, The Young Italian*), though, in the works of that author, the mysteries are always given some plausible explanation. Although most points in our scheme are not applicable to this story, the atmosphere and the whole conception of the theme of *The Prophetic Pictures* is nevertheless one of the most manifest examples of Hawthorne's close connection with the novel of terror and wonder.

Doctor Heidegger's Experiment (*Twice-told Tales*) was written in 1836. The old scientist here portrayed, and his surroundings, are repeatedly to be met with in Hawthorne's later productions. He is busy with chemical and magic experiments in his study, "a dim, old-fashioned chamber, festooned with cobwebs, and besprinkled with antique dust." There is a mirror, of which it is rumoured that all the doctor's deceased patients dwell within its verge and "would stare him in the face whenever he looked thitherward." We here find a further development of the idea expounded in the passage cited in the preceding paragraph. — There are also a bust of Hippocrates, a skeleton and a portrait of a young lady. Most marvellous of all, however, is Dr. Heidegger's book: "There were no letters on the back, and nobody could tell the title of the book. But it was well known to be a book of magic; and once, when a chambermaid had lifted it, merely to brush away the dust, the skeleton had rattled in its closet, the picture of the young lady had stepped one foot upon the floor, and several ghastly faces had peeped forth from the mirror; while the brazen head of Hippocrates frowned and said — "Forbear!"

In this room, we find, apart from the host, four guests of his, a lady and three gentlemen of his own age. All four of them are described in Hawthorne's accurate and amusing manner, and we likewise get an analytic description of their reactions when the host, producing a withered rose, dips it into a mysterious liquid that changes the shrivelled flower into a fresh bud and afterwards asks his guests to taste of the elixir that he has procured from the Fountain of Youth down in Florida. The first glass changes the four old people into middle-aged ones, the second transforms them into youths. They laugh and dance, and in the rivalry of courtship, the vase containing the precious fluid is dashed onto the floor. The whole scene is reflected in the mirror, which shows four elderly people in an unseemly intoxicated state. Gradually, the rose withers again, and three aged gentlemen and a matron are once more sitting round the table of their host. — "You have taught me a lesson," says Dr. Heidegger. — "I shall never taste the water from the Fountain of Youth."

There is no small part of the machinery of the Gothic novel to be found in this story. Dr. Heidegger must be viewed as a sort of modernized wizard (8), and his elixir as a witch beverage (8). In his room are to be found a skeleton (7), a magic mirror (11), a moving portrait, and a bust endowed with the power of speech (11). The whole of this didactic fantasy is built on a Gothic foundation. In a foot-note, Hawthorne meets certain accusations of having plagiarized the idea of the story from a chapter in one of the novels of Alexandre Dumas. He shows that his own tale was written several years before the publication of the work of the Frenchman. When speaking of the four unpublished posthumous manuscripts of Hawthorne, we shall have cause to revert to Dr. Heidegger and his cobwebby study.

In 1838, Hawthorne wrote four tales of old Boston and published them under the joint title of *Legends of the Province House* (*Twice-told Tales*). The Province House was the former mansion of the English governors of the town, and had, in

Hawthorne's day, been adapted as a public-house. We have already mentioned Washington Irving as a predecessor of Hawthorne's and the introducer of the Romantic short story into American literature. Like many of his European models, Irving liked to join the short stories together in a framework tale. According to Hawthorne's principal editor, T. P. Lathrop,[1] Hawthorne originally intended to provide such a framework for the *Twice-told Tales*, but gave up the plan. The four stories from the Province House, are, however, bound together in this way. Hawthorne tells us, how, on a summer's evening, he discovers the old house and enters it with a view to sightseeing. The detailed description of the house, which covers several pages, would do credit to the author of a guide-book; the whole manner reminds the reader of Hawthorne's English note-books and of *Our Old Home*, the work through which Hawthorne wanted to make his fellow-countrymen familiar with their mother-country. Hawthorne finally takes a seat in the bar-room, where Mr. Tiffany, an old customer and gossip, tells him the story of the festivity celebrated by governor Howe during the siege of Boston. "It is," says Hawthorne, "desperately hard work, when we attempt to throw the spell of hoar antiquity over localities with which the living world, and the day that is passing over us, have aught to do." But his attempt at evoking before the reader's eyes the last festival given by a British governor in the town of Boston, is a great success. Sir William Howe was the name of this dignitary, and the party he gave was a masquerade. The British guests were all very merry, but among them there was also to be discovered a very serious personage: old Colonel Joliffe, who belonged to the Whig party, has, strangely enough, accepted the governor's invitation. Eleven strokes had pealed from the old clock, when an unexpected music was heard from outside the house. The host frowned at the sound of the funeral march which had been played at the death of George III, but when he found that it was not his own orchestra that played it, he did nothing to stop the music In a little while, a strange procession was seen to descend the

---

[1] The Riverside Edition of Hawthorne's *Collected Works*.

great staircase. The foremost was a man in the old Puritan
garb with a steeple crowned hat and a skull-cap. — Endicott!
it was whispered among the crowd, and after him there followed
all the deceased governors and rulers of the old original de-
mocracy of Massachusetts, such as they had once wandered
about in their lifetime. Astonishment reached its peak, when
Howe's predecessor, Gage, advanced, just at the moment when
the light of the lamps began to flicker. After him followed a
shape, drawing up his military cloak over his face — the
likeness of Howe himself! The governor took a step forward,
but checked himself. It is said that the gesture made by his
double in that moment was exactly the same as the one Sir
William made some hours later when, for the last time, he
passed through the portal of the Province House. It was a
departed power that was commemorated by the ghostly procession.

Hawthorne makes the reader suspect that the whole event
may have been a bitter jest, arranged by old Joliffe. But the
description wholly tallies with the legend that Hawthorne had
also heard, that on each anniversary of the British defeat, all
the former governors of Massachusetts still glide through the
portal of the Province House. The flickering of the lamplights,
the sinister funeral march, and the procession itself, have a
decidedly supernatural character, not far removed from the world
of Mrs. Radcliffe. The reader is free to choose: either to believe in a ghostly apparition, or to view the whole pageant as
a macabre warning jest played by the Boston Whig party.
The method reminds one of Irving's manner, and some parts of
this story may also make the reader remember *The Masque of
the Red Death* by Edgar Allan Poe, which has certain affinities
with it.

The ghost-like atmosphere also pervades the three other
stories of the Province House. Number two of them, which is
also told by the elderly gentleman of the bar-room, is called
Edward Randolph's Portrait, and is centred round an old picture which has formerly hung in the Province House: "The
canvas itself was so dark with age, damp, and smoke, that not
a touch of the painter's art could be discerned. Time had

thrown an impenetrable veil over it, and left to tradition and fable and conjecture to say what had once been there portrayed." Some people state it to be an authentic portrait of the Evil One, others believe that a familiar spirit abides behind the blackness of the canvas and has shown himself, at seasons of calamity, to the governors. The governor who inhabits the house at the time of the story, Hutchinson, believes the picture to represent Edward Randolph, the builder of the house and the man who obtained the repeal of the first provincial charter, thus depriving the Bostonians of their democratic privileges. One evening, he tells this view to a young relative of his, Alice Vane, a pale, young lady who has been educated in Europe, and, among other things, has learned all the secrets of the art of painting. She suggests that it might be possible to remove the black surface of the canvas, but the discussion passes on to other subjects: the governor's decision to make British troops that are still on board a ship in the harbour, occupy a neighbouring fortress in order to subdue the rebellious colony. When Alice Vane bids her companions good night, her air and mien are "such as might have belonged to one of those spirits of fable — fairies or creatures of a more antique mythology — who sometimes mingled their agency with mortal affairs, half in caprice, yet with a sensibility to human weal or woe."

On the following morning, the landing of the troops, which is expected to cause serious trouble, is discussed in the Province House. Just as the governor lifts his pen to sign the fatal order, Alice Vane steps forward and draws aside a curtain that she has hung over the mysterious portrait. "By heaven," cries the governor, "if the spirit of Edward Randolph were to appear among us from the place of torment, he could not wear more of the terrors of hell upon his face."

In spite of this warning, Hutchinson signs the order — and burdens his conscience with a great guilt: "As, far over the ocean, his dying hour drew on, he gasped for breath, and complained that he was choking with the blood of the Boston Massacre." In his face there are traces of the same desperate expression that had characterized Randolph's portrait. It was

afterwards rumoured, that, during the night following upon the
fatal decision, the portrait had stepped out of its frame and
spoken face to face with the governor. But if such a miracle
had taken, place, it had left no trace, and the portrait was soon
afterwards once more covered with the impenetrable cloud that
had always veiled it. The effect of Alice Vane's method of
removing it — was it a painter's trick learnt in Italy, or some
witchery? — lasted only a few brief hours.

In this tale, which likewise leaves the reader to choose between belief in miracles and scepticism, we thus find a mysterious
portrait (11) that has been dexterously used to draw an historical
parallel. We further remark the words cited about the governor's feeling of being "choked with blood" (12) at the memory
of his guilty action, and the suggestion that Miss Vane's
manipulations with the picture might be of a supernatural kind
(8). But, on the other hand, what charming young lady might
not in the eighteen thirties be likened to a fairy?

Lady Eleanor's Mantle is the title of the third tale, which
is also told by the aforesaid Mr. Tiffany at a first-class oyster
supper in the Province House. Lady Eleanor was a young lady
belonging to the English aristocracy, who, at the beginning of
the 18th century, arrived on a visit to her relative, Colonel
Shute, at the time the resident in the Province House. Lady
Eleanor was a beauty, and her arrival was looked forward to
with a certain excitement, partly because it was said that an
embroidered mantle in her possession "was invested with magic
properties, so as to lend a new and untried grace to her figure
each time that she put it on." The garment was, according to
rumour, embroidered by a woman who had been waiting for
her own impending death. The governor arranged a festivity in
Lady Eleanor's honour, and the gorgeous mantle was admired
by everybody, while its bearer lost ever more sympathy through
her malicious sarcasms and haughty manner. Among the guests
at the party appeared a young man, Jervase Helwyse, whose
suit Eleanor had refused in England, and who had now followed
her to the New World. He offered her a cup of wine as "a
symbol that you have not sought to withdraw yourself from the
chain of human sympathies." He also asked her to throw off

the mantle. She refused, and he was led away. A short time afterwards, an epidemic disease broke out in the town; contrary to the normal course, it seemed at first to confine itself to the higher circles of society. Gradually, the infection was traced back to — Lady Eleanor's mantle. Jervase Helwyse went to see her, disfigured by the illness, and snatched away the fatal garment. Afterwards the people formed a procession, at the head of which was carried a puppet bearing the mantle. It is told that the plague disappeared when the puppet and the mantle had been burned, and that a mysterious woman bearing a wide mantle is still seen of nights in the Province House.

The witchery of this story of the magic mantle has travelled rather far from the manner of Washington Irving, and bears the true Hawthornesque stamp. It is not so far from the embroidered mantle to the embroidered A on Hester Prynne's breast. The theme is here less the historical ghost than the story of how the proud Lady Eleanor, who could feel no compassion with Jervase Helwyse, became in her turn the victim of somebody stronger than herself. The mantle becomes a symbol of her pride and of the punishment that the sinner carries with him. Still, we note number (7) of our list — the ghost of Lady Eleanor — and (8), the bewitched mantle of hers.

Old Esther Dudley, the fourth story of the Province House, tells of the last loyal British subject left in Boston after the departure of the last governor. Old Esther is a decayed descendant of an old English family who has found a refuge in the Province House and stays on there after Governor Howe and the British troops have left the town. She takes care of the old house and its treasures, among which there is a mysterious old mirror of which people tell that "old Esther could cause the Governors of the overthrown dynasty, with the beautiful ladies who had once adorned their festivals, the Indian chiefs who had come up to the Province House to hold council or swear allegiance, the grim Provincial warriors, the severe clergymen — in short, all the pageantry of bygone days — all the figures that ever swept across the broad plate of glass in former times — she could cause the whole to reappear and people the inner world of the mirror with shadows of old life." It was

rumoured that if she felt lonely, she was wont to summon a
black slave from the mirror and send him to fetch company
from the churchyard: "forth went the sable messenger with the
starlight or the moonshine gleaming through him, and did his
errand in the burial ground, knocking at the iron doors of
tombs or upon the marble slabs that covered them."

But the guests that are dearest to Old Esther Dudley are
the children of the town. She talks to them of bygone days,
and when they return to their homes, they will, in their turn,
tell stories of people of the past, as if they were still living.
They claim to have met a governor long since dead, but, they
say, "when old Esther Dudley had done speaking about him
he faded away out of his chair."

Time passes, and the Republican governor Hancock is
appointed and takes possession of the Province House. Old
Esther Dudley perceives that a festival occasion is at hand.
She arrays herself in her best silk and descends the great
staircase to kneel to the newcomer. "God save King George"
is her strange greeting when giving him the keys. And so the
representative of another aera dies as the new age crosses the
threshold of the Province House.

The ghostly atmosphere of this story is not as strong as in
the other three. The light over it has rather a sad lustre. It
is the superstition of her environment that partly isolates old
Esther Dudley. The old woman, who lives wholly in the past,
is understood only by the children: "Thus, without affrightening
her little guests, she led them by the hand into the chambers
of her own desolate heart, and made childhood's fancy discern
the ghosts that haunted there." But the machinery is easily
recognized. The magic mirror (11), the moon that shines through
the ghostly negro (9), the whole idea of nocturnal banquets
where the whole party is called forth from the mirror and have
their domiciles in the churchyard (7), all these conceptions are
so many borrowings from the world of terror and wonder.
"Weird" is the word used by Lathrop about these historical
tales, which are typical of Hawthorne's attempts to invest the
past of his country with life. Unlike the European Romanticists
or their great model, Shakespeare, he had no medieval history

to revive, but the same dim and mysterious twilight that they had borrowed from age-old legends and popular superstition in their countries was searched for by him in the comparatively recent beginnings of the New World and spread over his tales.

The sorcerers of the Middle Ages, with their alchemy and their faculty of infusing life into the pictures they painted, might seem to an imaginative person of the eighteen thirties to be reborn in the chemists and photographers of the new time. That the practitioners of both these professions were, in Hawthorne's opinion, surrounded by a radiance of mysticism, is proved over and over again by his works. I have chosen two representative short stories to illustrate this fact: *The Birthmark* (1843) and *Rappacini's Daughter* (1843), both included in *Mosses from an Old Manse*.

The Birthmark is the tale of the beautiful Georgiana, the perfect woman, who, at the end of the 18th century, just "when the comparatively recent discovery of Nature seemed to open paths into the region of miracle" has been married to Aylmer, the eminent man of science. Georgiana's beauty has but one blemish: a birthmark in the shape of a tiny hand appears on her cheek when she blushes. In order to be absolutely faultless in the eyes of Aylmer, Georgiana suffers him to make her the object of a scientific experiment to remove the stain on her beauty. Georgiana is introduced into Aylmer's laboratory, where his assistant Aminadab, a sort of Caliban, is working: "With his vast strength, his shaggy hair, his smoky aspect, and the indescribable earthiness that incrusted him, he seemed to represent man's physical nature." Georgiana is placed in a beautiful apartment, specially arranged for the occasion, and unconsciously becomes the object of mysterious influences from the adjoining laboratory. Finally, Aylmer offers her the magic potion. Georgiana falls asleep, and the birthmark slowly fades away. When she awakes, however, it is only to find that she is going to die. The fatal hand has grappled with the mystery of life in her. Aminadab chuckles hoarsely. The gross being of the earth knows well that men cannot with immunity seek perfection in human existence.

The second tale, *Rappacini's Daughter,* is in the introduction

said to be written by a Frenchman, Monsieur de l'Aubépine.
The pseudonym is intentionally transparent, and we have already
paid attention to the self-characterization given by Hawthorne
in this connection. The story itself has its setting in Padua,
whither a young Italian, Giovanni Guasconti, comes in order to
pursue his medical studies. When he has moved into his lod-
gings, he discovers in the garden of the adjoining house a
beautiful young maiden who wanders about among the most
wonderful flowers. Her father is Professor Rappacini, a scientist
who lives isolated from his colleagues because his scientific zeal
is so ruthless that he shows no regard for human considerations
when he wishes to obtain scientific results. In his garden he
cultivates strange and venomous plants. He dare not touch
them himself, but his daughter Beatrice has grown up among
them and is wholly imbued with their fragrant potency. Guasconti and Beatrice fall in love with each other, and often meet
in the garden, in spite of the warnings of Guasconti's old
teacher. One day, this old man tells the youth everything about
Rappacini and his perilous experiments, and Guasconti is horrified
to find that he, too, has been imbued with the poisons of Rappacini's garden. Flowers fade in his hands, insects die when
they meet his breath. He descends to keep a tryst with Beatrice, carrying with him a flagon with a strong antidote. Beatrice seizes it, drinks the liquor and sinks down upon the ground.
"Thus the poor victim of man's ingenuity and of thwarted
nature, and of the fatality that attends all such efforts of per-
verted wisdom, perished . . ."

Both of these stories are enacted in a world of quasi-scientific
experiments that is rather remote from the Gothic novel. But
in the later varieties of it, e. g. Melmoth, we find the man of
science, who has plighted himself to the devil, who occupies
himself with alchemy or the interpreting of old documents and
in whose study skeletons and crystal globes are to be found.
Features of the Faust figure, of Macchiavelli and the Wandering
Jew are to be traced in these old magicians. In spite of his
youth, Aylmer is a typical sorcerer of this kind (4). His sub-
ordinate Aminadab has, apart from his name, other features
drawn from the Oriental novel, while in outward appearance

he resembles the misshapen villain (6). Rappacini himself is not only a deeply immoral scientist but, furthermore, an Italian (4, 5). The devil's elixir (8) has acquired a new and original shape in this story, and the old manuscript (2) is nothing less than the collected works of Monsieur de l'Aubépine. If Hawthorne was elsewhere fully conscious of using the machinery of Gothic romance, it is possible that in this case he was not aware of it. We shall not enter here upon the genesis and symbolism of these two stories, which have been made the object of exhaustive researches by other authors.[1]

The story which has given its title to the collection *The Snow Image and Other Tales* (1847), also contains an element of wonder, which must not be left out in the present connection. It bears the sub-title "A Childish Miracle," and describes how a snow figure, modelled by two little playing children, is endowed with life and becomes their playmate. Hawthorne got the idea of this story when he saw his own children romping in the snow, and it is one of the most charming examples of his exceptional talent for depicting children. It possesses both humour and poetry, and a slightly pathetic moral. The little snow-girl is not allowed to remain in her own element: the kind and sensitive father of the children drags her into the house to get her warm in front of the fire. The lesson to be learned is "that it behoves man, and especially men of benevolence, to consider well what they are about, and, before acting on their philanthropic purposes, to be quite sure that they comprehend the nature and all relations of the business in hand." There is no gloomy Gothic mysticism in this airy play of fantasy. It is a fairy-tale, in which the children introduce into the every-day life of quite a common family a miracle, in the person of the enchanting little snow-image. When the mother looks out through the window, there is "a small figure of a girl, dressed in white with rose-tinged cheeks and ringlets of golden hue, playing about the garden with the two children . . . airily as she was clad, the child seemed to feel not the slightest inconvenience from the cold, but danced so lightly over the snow that the

---

[1] Dhaleine, *N. Hawthorne, sa vie et son œuvre.* Paris, 1905.

tips of her toes left hardly a print on its surface." Real though
the charming little image is, she never opens her lips to utter
a word, and when she enters and is placed in front of the hearth,
she simply thaws, dissolving into a little puddle of water.

We here find ourselves far removed from armour, Gothic
castles, and bloods-tains. The supernatural feature of the story
is the fact that the little image awakens to life. A similar motive, worked out in a far more traditional manner, is employed
in *Feathertop* (1848, *Mosses from an Old Manse*). Its sub-title is
"A Moralized Legend," and the structure and manner of the
story remind the reader of old European popular stories of the
kind collected by the brothers Grimm. "Upon my word," says
Hawthorne in the introductory paragraph, "if the legend were
not one which I heard on my grandmother's knee, and which
had established its place among things credible before my childish
judgment could analyse its possibilities, I question whether I
should have the face to tell it now."[1]

The contents of the story are as follows: Mother Rigby calls
for her invisible servant Dickon to get a coal to light her pipe.
She then begins to create or rather manufacture a scarecrow
out of a broomstick, a flail, a puddingstick, a meal bag, and a
pumpkin. When it is ready, it is named Feathertop, and acquires
life through a puff at Mother Rigby's pipe. And so she sends
Feathertop out into the world to make his own fortune. His
life depends on the pipe; he must constantly puff at it, and
now and then get it lighted anew by calling Dickon. Feathertop
arrives in the town, where he is very much honoured, and
under the name of Lord Feathertop he pays his respects to
Master Gookin and his pretty daughter Polly, who is on the
verge of falling in love with him. But suddenly she catches
sight of him in a mirror, and shrieks. Feathertop likewise looks
towards the mirror, and there beholds "not the glittering mockery
of his outside show, but a picture of the sordid patchwork of
his real composition, stripped of all witchcraft." Mother Rigby

---

[1] Concerning the lively discussion of Hawthorne's dependence on Tieck
in this special case, I refer the reader to the results of the researches made
by Schönbach, Belden and Just to which I have already drawn attention.
Cp. pp. 15 & 28.

is sitting at her hearth, puffing away at her pipe, when Feather-top returns. He does not feel like living any longer. The fault is not Polly's, nor anybody else's: "I've seen myself for the wretched, ragged, empty thing I am," he says. And so Feather-top becomes at last only a scarecrow.

Here we find once more a rich flora of elements from the world of the Gothic novel and the supernatural world. Mother Rigby is a hag (8) with an invisible servant of a devilish nature (4). Feathertop is admired by many people, akin with the good citizens of the town where H. C. Andersens's emperor with the invisible clothes lived: they are willing to be swindled, though the dog barks at Feathertop, and a little child prattles "some unintelligible nonsense about a pumpkin." The mirror, which is incapable of flattery, exposes Feathertop's whole piti-fulness (11).

After *Feathertop*, Hawthorne wrote only two more short stories before passing over to the romances. To the reader of to-day, the short stories of Hawthorne often seem to have re-tained more of their freshness than his longer works. This may certainly be partly explained by his manner of applying the machinery of Gothic romance in the different instances. The very details that may in a short and artistic pastiche be of good effect, even because of their fantastic nature, will easily make his larger canvases appear rather affected and give them an antiquated stamp. But though one may be tempted to smile at the supernatural fancies and the host of reminiscences from Radcliffe and Mathurin in the novels of Hawthorne, one ends by finding them indispensable. They form an integral and es-sential element of his artistic method, and a great part of his originality consists in his completely unprejudiced manner of using old, worn-out ideas and figures abstracted from Gothic literature which had entered into the common imagination of the reading public. As we have partly been able to de-monstrate while analyzing his short stories, the central problem that pervades most of his work is, however, a purely psycholo-gical question: the rôle of sin in human life. It formed the main theme of *The Scarlet Letter* which appeared in 1850. I shall give a short synopsis of the action of this novel.

In one of the earliest immigration years, Hester Prynne has arrived, alone and unknown, in the town of Boston. After some time it becomes known that she is expecting a child, but she refuses to reveal the identity of its father. She is put into prison and there gives birth to a girl, who is called Pearl. The romance opens with Hester's coming out of prison. According to the sentence of the magistrates, she has to stand on the scaffold as a penitent, and afterwards she must always wear on her bosom a red letter A (signifying Adulteress) sewn on to her dress. Hester submits to the judgment, but endeavours to render the token of her sin as beautiful as possible. Her fingers are deft and skilful, and the red letter, which estranges her from her intolerant environment, glows in brilliant red and golden hues of silk embroidery. As gorgeous as the letter is little Pearl. The children are in general exempted from the Puritan insistence on black clothing, and the girl is beautifully dressed in the same colours as the token on her mother's bosom. Time passes, and Hester Prynne leads an exemplary life, taking care of the sick and earning her living as a seamstress.

On the very day when Hester came out of prison, there arrived in the town an elderly man, who turns out to be a skilful physician and calls himself Chillingworth. Among his patients is the young minister of the town, Dimmesdale, who has a great reputation as a future spiritual leader, as well on account of his sermons, where penitence for hidden sins is one of the most frequent themes, as because of his ascetic way of life. In the description of all these things, the chief stress is put on the slow inner process through which Dimmesdale, who is the father of Hester Prynne's child, is driven to public confession. Under the pretence of medical attendance, Chillingworth, who, in fact, is Hester's husband, with a devilish mixture of deep-rooted ill-will and scientific thoroughness, drives him on to increasing self-torture. The principal persons are, consequently, the two sinners, Hester and Dimmesdale, and the victims, Chillingworth and Pearl.

According to the traditional Puritan view, the course of events ought to be arranged so that the sinners are punished, and the victims obtain satisfaction. But to Hawthorne's mind, the greatest guilt does not belong to those who have sinned against the commandments of the moral code. "What we did had a consecration of its own," says Hester to Dimmesdale. To Hester, the isolation caused by the red letter on her bosom becomes the spur to a richer development of her personality. If the well-to-do and robust people around her shut their doors to the excommunicated sinner, the poor and sick instead open theirs to the modest and skilful nurse. She has found her life's path, and when, after the confession, she chooses to remain in New England, continuing her work of charity there she becomes, in spite of the red letter, a generally esteemed woman — Hawthorne shuns overstatements, but the reader may possibly feel tempted to discern a faint halo around her saint-like head.

Dimmesdale follows another course. Without confessing his crime, he tries to atone for it by continuing and intensifying his religious work, But here, it seems that the commandment of first removing the beam from one's own eye must be applied with Puritan severity. He does not feel at peace with himself till he has publicly ascended the scaffold of the pillory together with Hester and little Pearl. It is Dimmesdale's route from the pulpit to the pillory that occupies the greatest space in the book, and engrosses most of the author's interest. With unyielding and minute exactitude he follows the development of Dimmesdale's consciousness of sin, which is also symbolized by an A, branded on his bosom but concealed from the eyes of the multitude. Many readers and critics have expressed their dissatisfaction with the lack of explanation of the real nature of this letter. Was it a form of stigmatization, as palpable to other humans as to Dimmesdale himself, or was it a fantasy, produced by his sick conscience? Was it perhaps the symptom of a physical disease, which had, by a whim of fate, taken a form resembling Hester Prynne's scarlet letter? Or was it the effect of the treatment which Chillingworth had given the minister? These questions are never answered. The scarlet letter is a symbol, or perhaps rather an allegory, that pervades the whole book. It is to be found on Hester Prynne's garment, it burns on Dimmesdale's breast, it flames as a menacing omen in the sky during the scene by night when Hester and Dimmesdale meet at the scaffold, and it is personified in little Pearl, who, in her clothes of red and gold, seems to be not an earthly child but some elfish, or rather impish, sprite.

In fact, little Pearl, who is one of the victims of the sin, is nothing but a living accusation. There exists a mysterious connection between her and the letter on her mother's bosom, not only visible in her own appearance, but also inherent in her demeanour; as a baby she reaches for it, and when a little older, she often looks at the letter when speaking to her mother, and likes to draw attention to it. When Hester and Dimmesdale finally meet in the forest and Hester tears away the sign and throws it away among the trees, Pearl finds it again and carries it back to her mother. Pearl does not become a real human child till the confession has taken place. We are told that afterwards she grows up and becomes a beautiful young lady in a far-off country, where she even marries a nobleman and naturally always keeps up contact with her mother in the little Puritan town over the Ocean.

The fourth principal person, Chillingworth, plays the darkest rôle in this gloomy story. He is also the bearer of a guilt which consists in his having married Hester not because of her personality but because of her beauty. The conception that beauty is a great difficulty and danger, not to say a misfortune, to a woman, especially if she chance also to possess brains and heart, is peculiar to Hawthorne, and has been stressed by his French biographer.[1] But Chillingworth does not choose the path of confession and atonement. Instead, he sinks deeper and deeper in dark thoughts of implacability and vengeance, and the consequence is his own disaster.

The student who leaves out of consideration the chief problems concerned with the development of characters — which would otherwise constitute a tempting theme for a closer investigation — and concentrates his attention on the traces of Gothic romance to be found in *The Scarlet Letter*, will be able to gather a not inconsiderable fund of observations.[2] In the

[1] Dhaleine, *N. Hawthorne, sa vie et son œuvre.* Paris, 1905. Cp. Zenobia *(A Blithedale Romance)* and Miriam *(The Marble Faun).*

[2] For the results of my investigations concerning the reminiscences of Gothic Romance to be found in *The Scarlet Letter* and *The House of the*

preface to the book, which is regarded as a masterpiece of satire, where Hawthorne has unburdened himself of the disgust and irritation that had accumulated in his mind during the years spent in the Customs House at Salem, he states that he got the idea for the novel from an old manuscript found among a heap of rubbish in an attic in the Customs House. In the roll of parchment, there was also "a certain affair or fine red cloth, much worn and faded" — nothing less than the famous Scarlet Letter. Hawthorne even tells us that he tried to fasten it on his own breast, and thereby "experienced a sensation not altogether physical, yet almost so, as of burning heat; and as if the letter were not of red cloth but red-hot iron."

Here, then, we find the classical source of the Gothic novel: the manuscript (1), and an amulet with more or less pronounced magical qualities (8). Looking for an equivalent to (2) in our list, the Gothic castle, to our astonishment we discover such a one in the heart of seventeenth-century Boston. When Hester and Pearl one day go to visit Governor Bellingham, the man is found residing in a house that is built of wood, but covered by a kind of stucco in which fragments of broken glass are intermixed and where "cabalistic figures and diagrams" have been engraved. There are also narrow towers on each side of the arched entrance. The interior, likewise, reveals many tokens of mediaeval times. The huge hall is illuminated by a bow-window with a deep and cushioned seat, the table and chairs are heirlooms "of the Elizabethan age or perhaps earlier," on the walls there hangs a row of stern portraits, and, finally, we find a suit of mail with a burnished breastplate standing before the oak panelling. Here, we recognize the traditional armour (10), which also serves another end: little Pearl uses it as a looking-glass (11) where "owing to the peculiar effect of this convex mirror" Hester's scarlet letter is "represented in exaggerated and gigantic proportions, so as to be greatly the most prominent feature of her appearance." Number (3) — the mysterious crime — is represented by the guilt of Hester and

---

Seven Gables, I am indebted to impulses and observations given by Professor S. B. Liljegren in his lecture on *The American Novel of Terror*, October 12th, 1944.

Dimmesdale, and Dimmesdale's position as a minister invests the crime with the religious character so dear to Gothic romance. The mental sapping work of Chillingworth may also be counted as a crime (3). His deformity (6) has already been mentioned.[1] Hawthorne repeatedly takes his readers to the cemetery of Boston (7). There, Chillingworth finds some of his mysterious herbs: "I found them (answered the physician) growing on a grave, which bore no tombstone, nor other memorial of the dead man, save these ugly weeds, that have taken upon themselves to keep him in remembrance. They grew out of his heart, and typify, it may be, some hideous secret that was buried with him, and which he had done better to confess during his life-time." Little Pearl feels very much at home in the burial ground. She speaks of the Black Man who is coming to fetch her mother and the minister. "So she drew her mother away, skipping, dancing and frisking fantastically, among the hillocks of the dead people, like a creature that had nothing in common with a bygone and buried generation, nor owned herself akin to it. It was as if she had been made afresh, out of new elements . . ." Hags (8) are mentioned in several instances. The sister of the Governor, Mrs. Hibbins, is a hag, a fact that is repeatedly and expressly stressed. Mrs. Hibbins is wont to speak of the witches' meetings in the forest: "Ha, ha, ha, cackled the old witch-lady, still nodding her high head-dress at the minister . . . Well, well, we must needs talk thus in the day-time. You carry it off like an old hand. But at midnight, and in the forest, we shall have other talk together." Chillingworth's rôle as a magician is proved by his interest not only in healing herbs but also in alchemy: "Old Chillingworth arranged his laboratory not such as a modern man of science would reckon even tolerably complete, but provided with a distilling apparatus and the means of compounding drugs and chemicals which the practised alchemist knew well how to turn to purpose." During his Indian captivity he has also "enlarged his medical attainments by joining in the incantations of the savage priests; who were universally acknowledged to be powerful en-

---

[1] Cp. p. 26, note.

chanters, often performing seemingly miraculous cures by their skill in the black art."

We have already spoken of the magic letter A, which must also be included under (8), and about its appearance as an omen in the sky, which must belong under (9) of our list. The A on Dimmesdale's breast is never fully explained, but there are hints that it might be regarded as a case of stigmatization (4). Concerning the mirrors (11) there are some further observations to be added. When Hester longs to see her own image reflected in Pearl's eye, she perceives "not her own miniature portrait, but another face . . . fiend-like, full of malice, yet bearing the semblance of features that she had known full well, though seldom with a smile, and never with malice in them. It was as if an evil spirit possessed the child, and had just then peeped forth in mockery." With his accustomed evasiveness, Hawthorne shuns a closer analysis of what Hester really saw. Perhaps it was a revelation of a likeness between the child and her father, which made her think of his constant remorse. However, this mirror effect is very impressive. Another effect of the same kind is attained when Hawthorne describes little Pearl impishly playing about in the wood. The child stands before a little pool which reflects her figure: "This image, so nearly identical with the living Pearl, seemed to communicate somewhat of its own shadowy and intangible quality to the child herself."

The examples of the use of Gothic machinery in *The Scarlet Letter* might be multiplied, but these specimens of ten of the twelve items on our list seem to suffice for supporting the assertion that Hawthorne in his first full-length novel shows himself to be heavily indebted to the authors of the old novels of terror and wonder.

As early as 1851, Hawthorne published his second novel, *The House of the Seven Gables*. Reminiscences from his native town and old stories from the family chronicle of the Hawthornes' provide a great deal of the material for this work, the theme of which is the psychological study of a supposed crime and its consequence for members of two families.

The old house that forms the scene of the action, and at the same time is a symbol of the disastrous power and influence of family tradition, was built in the seventeenth century by the hard and ruthless Colonel Pyncheon on a piece of soil which he had wrongfully usurped from the poor carpenter Matthew Maule. When, some years later, Matthew Maule was accused of sorcery and hanged, he cursed the whole family of the Pyncheons and prophesied that the Colonel would "get blood to drink." The Colonel, who was said to have acquired a large and fertile piece of land from an Indian tribe, later died under dramatic circumstances, with a stream of blood trickling from his mouth. His heirs in vain sought for the document by which the purchase had been confirmed. Of the Maule family it was only known that Matthew's son had assisted at the building of the House of the Seven Gables, and it was believed that the family became extinct at his death. The Pyncheon family, on the other hand, flourished during two centuries more. Once, about thirty years before the beginning of the story, an old bachelor, who was of an eccentric turn of mind, wanted to restore the house to its rightful owners, if any members of the Maule family were to be found; but before he had been able to realize these plans, the old man was found dead, possibly the victim of a murderer. His nephew Clifford was accused of the deed, and he received the death-sentence, later on commuted to imprisonment for life. Another nephew, who showed in his character all the traditional ruthlessness of the Pyncheons, and who was also an image of the old Colonel as to his outer appearance, inherited the fortune of his uncle. At the beginning of the story, twenty years after the violent death of the old man, this nephew of his, Judge Pyncheon, has become an important citizen in the little town, and Clifford's sister, Hepzibah, resides in the family mansion. In order to earn her living, she has sublet a couple of rooms to a young daguerrotypist, Holgrave, and she also opens a little cent-shop in the basement story of the house, some days before she expects her brother Clifford, who has been released, to return home. Just at that moment she receives an unexpected visit from a distant relative, the young Phoebe Pyncheon. Phoebe is as gay and lively as she is simple and charming; she fills the old house with life and runs the cent-shop in a splendid manner. When Clifford arrives, tired and worn-out by the long prison years, she becomes indispensable to him, and Holgrave falls in love with her.

After some time, Phoebe departs, and a little later, Judge Pyncheon presents himself and asks to see Clifford, stating that the old man must possess some knowledge of where the family fortune is to be found, thereby alluding to the lost Indian contract. The Judge places himself in an old family chair, according to tradition the very one in which the Colonel was once found dead, and under a portrait of that ancestor, which is strikingly like himself. Clifford has disappeared, but then suddenly presents himself, and at this surprise, the Judge gets such a shock, that he collapses in the chair and dies. Clifford and Hepzibah are very much frightened — Clifford has once before been accused of the murder of a member of the family who died in the selfsame room — and they depart on a fantastic flight by railway.

Phoebe returns and finds the house locked, but is let in through a back door by Holgrave. This young man now shows himself to be a descendant of Matthew Maule, from whom he has inherited something of the "mesmerism" that made the old "wizard" suspected of sorcery. He is also filled with radical ideas and interested in scientific experiments. He now declares that the judge, as well as his uncle previously — who had not really been murdered, but only severely frightened — and very likely the Colonel Pyncheon of yore, had all died from a hereditary disorder. Through a misunderstanding, the reason for which was known only to the Judge, Clifford had been accused of the murder of the old bachelor, and afterwards sentenced to imprisonment. Hepzibah and Clifford return, and everything is cleared up. Holgrave and Phoebe become engaged, and he builds a new house for them to live in. One day, he discloses the secret of his family. The carpenter Maule, who assisted at the building of the house of the seven gables, had hidden the Indian document, that would have procured so great riches to the Pyncheon family, in a secret niche behind the old family portrait. It is now so old as to have lost its validity. The old family feud is ended, and Phoebe and Holgrave begin their life in their new home with Hepzibah and Clifford, who also move from the dismal old house of the seven gables.

As is shown by this synopsis, the action of the novel is very insignificant. The dramatic events have taken place before the opening of the story, and the interest is centred on the character-drawing. There is no principal character in the proper sense of the word, if Clifford, the sensitive, unjustly accused victim, who late in life recovers his liberty, but must be considered a broken man, is not to be viewed as such. Holgrave, the representative of the new age and at the same time possessor of the personal magnetism that characterized his ancestor, the sorcerer, is an attempt to amalgamate old beliefs in magic with the interest in the secret faculties of the soul that was so generally prevalent in Hawthorne's time. Phoebe personifies the unspoilt freshness of youth, Hepzibah is a dried-up branch of an old tree. Judge Pyncheon embodies selfish greed and ruthlessness. The whole of the action is laid in modern times. Is it then possible to find any traces of Gothic romance in this story of an American family mansion of 1850? We shall pass on to a closer investigation of this interesting question.

The old house where the story is enacted and which has given the book its title is a dark and gloomy edifice. According to G. P. Lathrop,[1] there are in Salem at least three houses with claims to the honour of being the original of Hawthorne's house of the seven gables. But, as Hawthorne declares in his introduction, the mansion is first and foremost an edifice "of materials long in use for constructing castles in the air." According to the description in the opening chapter of the book, it rises in pride, not modesty, and its whole visible exterior is "ornamented with quaint figures, conceived in the grotesqueness of a Gothic fancy, and drawn or stamped in the glittering plaster, composed of lime, pebbles, and bits of glass, with which the woodwork of the walls is overspread." The medieval impression is enhanced by the seven pointed gables, which present "the aspect of a whole sisterhood of edifices," as by the principal entrance, which has "almost the breadth of a

---

[1] G. P. Lathrop, Introductory note to *The House of the Seven Gables*, Riverside Edition.

churchdoor." The psychic atmosphere of the house is perhaps best described by citing Clifford's assertion that "the greatest possible stumbling-block in the path of human happiness and improvement are these heaps of bricks and stones, consolidated with mortar, or hewn timber, fastened together with spike-nails, which men painfully contrive for their own torment, and call them house and home ... Morbid influences, in a thousand-fold variety, gather about hearths, and pollute the life of households. There is no such unwholesome atmosphere as that of an old home, rendered poisonous by one's defunct forefathers and relatives ... a rusty, crazy, creaky, dry-rotted, damp-rotted, dingy, dark and miserable old dungeon." It is not only the word dungeon that is here fetched from the Gothic mansions; also the peaked pinnacles and the quaint figures, expressly termed Gothic are devised to awake reminiscences from the reading of Gothic romance and catch something of the weird atmosphere belonging to it. Thus, we here note an instance of point (2) in our scheme.

The mysterious crime (3) appears in a very central position in this novel. It is represented by the repeated, unexplained deaths in the Pyncheon family, which for a long time remain unsolved riddles engendering evil deeds like Matthew Maule's hanging or Clifford's imprisonment. Colonel Pyncheon's acquisition of poor Maule's soil and the selfish and ruthlesss, not to say criminal, way in which the Judge takes possession of his uncle's papers and fortune are also actions fraught with disastrous consequences which may be included in this category.

The house of the seven gables and the happenings within its walls naturally give birth to a lot of rumours, and even if Hawthorne declares that he is speaking of local sayings, he delights in describing the ghostly happenings that are said to occur in the old building. An eighteenth century member of the family, who was the first to open the little shop in the basement, is, according to tradition, sometimes still visible there: "It used to be affirmed, that the dead shop-keeper in a white wig, a faded velvet coat, an apron at his waist, and his ruffles carefully turned back from his wrists, might be seen through the chinks of the shutters ... From the look of unutterable woe

upon his face, it appeared to be his doom to spend eternity in
a vain effort to make his accounts balance." It is also averred,
that the whole company of deceased members of the family
sometimes honour the house by visiting it: " . . . first comes the
ancestor himself, in his black cloak, steeple-hat, and trunk-
breeches, girt about the waist with a leathern belt, in which
hangs his steel-hilted sword . . . So decided is his look of dis-
content as to impart additional distinctness to his features,
through which, nevertheless, the moonlight passes, and flickers
on the wall beyond . . . Here comes other Pyncheons, the whole
tribe, in their half a dozen generations . . ." The beautiful Alice
Pyncheon, who fell into a tragic dependence on a witchcraft-
practising member of the Maule family, is also supposed to
haunt the house — "especially when one of the Pyncheons was
to die, she had been heard playing sadly and beautifully on
the harpsichord" and, true enough, Hepzibah catches a strain
of music immediately before the decease of Judge Pyncheon.
The ghostly music is a trait beloved especially by Mrs. Radcliffe.
The woods around the French châteaux in *The Mysteries of
Udolpho* resound ever and anon to harmonies of the same
melancholy and ghostly character as the preludes of Alice
Pyncheon's harpsichord.

We need not hesitate in classifying the members of the
Maule family with the community of sorcerers and magicians
(8). Even Holgrave's modern profession, that of a photographer,
is endowed with a magic and prophetic touch when Hawthorne
speaks of it.[1] It is said of the Maules, that "their companions . . .
grew conscious of a circle round about the Maules, within the
sanctity or the spell of which, in spite of an exterior of suffi-
cient frankness and good-fellowship, it was impossible for any
man to step . . . Among other good-for-nothing properties and
privileges, one was especially assigned them — that of exercising
an influence over people's dreams." This characterization may
be stretched a point to include also the mesmerism which
appertains to the late descendant of the Maules, Holgrave.
But every possibility of linking popular sayings with reality is

---

[1] Cp. p. 51.

excluded when it comes to the excellent specimens of ghosts drawn by Hawthorne in another description of the peculiarities of the Maule family, which is put in the mouth, or rather included in the manuscript, of Holgrave: "Their graves, in the crevices of rocks, were supposed to be incapable of retaining the occupants, who had been so hastily thrust into them. Old Matthew Maule, especially, was known to have as little hesitation or difficulty in rising out of his grave as an ordinary man in getting out of bed, and was as often seen at midnight as living people at noonday." It would be difficult to find a more accurate and at the same time humourously sceptical description of a real, old-time wizard ghost than this. Holgrave's sorcery is of a more modern kind. He makes pictures out of sunshine by means of his camera. But his pictures have a wonderful character of their own; there is, he says, "a wonderful insight in Heaven's broad and simple sunshine. While we give it credit only for depicting the merest surface, it actually brings out the deepest secret character with a truth that no painter would even venture upon, even could he detect it." The young man also possesses other mysterious qualities. "I am," says he to Phoebe, "somewhat of a mystic, it must be confessed. The tendency is in my blood, together with the faculty of mesmerism, which might have brought me to Gallow's Hill, in the good old times of witchcraft." A better expression of Hawthorne's view of old-time sorcery could not be found. He clearly perceived the identity of what his ancestors had termed witch-craft with phenomena that in his own days had found a scientific or at least pseudo-scientific explanation. But he preferred by far to use the old and romantic words and view-points in order to describe them and thus create the mysterious twilight in which his personages felt best at their ease and best could express the truths that he wanted to impress upon his readers.

An important rôle is also played by the ancestral chair (8) of the Pyncheons, of which it is once said that "it really seems to be enchanted like the one in Comus." Sitting in that same chair, the Colonel, the old unmarried uncle of Clifford, and Judge Pyncheon all get their mysterious attacks, or, as expressed in the language of superstition, "get blood to drink."

Above the chair hangs the picture of Colonel Pyncheon, the stern, unmitigable features of which "seemed to symbolize an evil influence, and so darkly to mingle the shadow of their presence with the sunshine of the passing hour, that no good thought or purposes could ever spring up and blossom there." In telling the legend of Alice Pyncheon, Holgrave also recounts what is rumoured of the old portrait: "This picture, it must be understood, was supposed to be so intimately connected with the fate of the house, and so magically built into its walls, that, if once it would be removed, that very instant the whole edifice would come thundering down in a heap of dusty ruin. All through the foregoing conversation between Mr. Pyncheon and the carpenter (Maule), the portrait had been frowning, clenching its fist, and giving many such proofs of excessive discomposure... And finally... the ghostly portrait is averred to have lost all patience, and to have shown itself on the point of descending bodily from its frame." Here, Hawthorne has given a free rein to his Gothic imagination and has gone almost as far as Walpole did in *The Castle of Otranto*. But it must be remarked, that this is not done in his own story, but in the old legend, which he makes Holgrave read aloud to Phoebe. We note, however, here a reminiscence of number (11) of our list.

Hawthorne's predilection for mirrors (11) is also visible here. The saying goes that in one room of the old house there hangs "a large, dim-looking glass... which was fabled to contain within its depths all the shapes that had ever been reflected there — the old colonel himself and his many descendants." In a different place, Hawthorne states that "the posterity of Matthew Maule had some connection with the mystery of the looking-glass, and that, by what appears to have been a sort of mesmeric process, they could make its inner region all alive with the departed Pyncheons." We recognize here a mirror of exactly the same kind as the one in the old Province House, where Esther Dudley used to surround herself with a mirror-bred society of bygone generations. In the novel of the Pyncheon family, however, the mirror never comes to play the rôle which seems designed for it in the description cited above.

The ancestral portrait has a central importance of a different kind for the plot of the book. In its frame there is a secret spring devised by the carpenter of the Maule family. The spring is known only to members of that "mesmeric" race, and it is by touching it that Holgrave finally brings forth the old document of the Indian sagamores, by which the Colonel had become entitled to such wide domains, now irreparably lost to his descendants. The portrait and the mirror may amply suffice to illustrate number (11) in our tabulation.

Number (12) is also represented in *The House of the Seven Gables*. The blood which God gives the members of the Pyncheon family to drink as a retribution for their sins is of a decidedly Gothic brand (12). The reader of Hawthorne's short stories may remember that Hutchinson, the British governor depicted in *Edward Randolph's Portrait*, when his dying hour drew on[1] "gasped for breath, and complained that he was choking with the blood of the Boston Massacre."

The House of the Seven Gables has more of a ghostly atmosphere than any other of the full-length stories that Hawthorne published during his life-time. The musty, dark, morbid and melancholy air throughout the book is temporarily blown away only by Phoebe's gay and girlish figure. The hatred of family oppression which pervades the whole work has certainly something to do with Hawthorne's own seclusion in his maternal home. Clifford's anathema over the family mansion may court comparison with passages from Ibsen's *Ghosts* or Samuel Butler's *The Way of All Flesh* of many decades later. But realism had not yet come into its own, and Hawthorne chose the tools that were at hand. The effects that he achieved by using parables and hints drawn from his reading as a schoolboy of the blood-curdling ghoststories, are still impressive in their subtle toning down and perfection of style.

A Blithedale Romance is the literary outcome of Hawthorne's stay at Brook Farm and his closer contact with the group of Transcendentalists who there sought the realization of a socialistic ideal. As has already been mentioned, Hawthorne found

---

[1] Cp. p. 47.

that for him rural labour was incompatible with literary activity.
He was a dreamer who shrank from practical life and soon got
tired of hard physical labour, however attractive the accom-
panying intellectual environment might seem to him. But his
disillusion was even deeper. He was a greater sceptic than
most of the idealistic "farm-hands" in the community and saw
clearly that the experiment could not be a lasting one. The
Blithedale Romance is perhaps first and foremost a settling of
his account with Brook Farm and with an exaggerated refor-
matory zeal, such as he has embodied it in the person of
Hollingsworth. His contemporaries already believed the fictitious
persons to be portraits of members of the Transcendentalist
group. Such insinuations were, however, consistently rejected
by Hawthorne.

When the narrator of the story, Miles Coverdale, who has
not a few features in common with Hawthorne himself, arrives
at Blithedale, he is met by the host, Silas Foster, and Zenobia,
the feminine soul of the enterprise. Zenobia's origin is obscure,
but she has created a position and a name for herself, as an
authoress and an artist in conversation. She is also very rich
and strikingly beautiful. Even in the simple dress that she is
wearing in this rural surrounding, her appearance is that of a
queen, and she gives a personal touch to her attire by always
wearing a sumptuous flower stuck into her black curls. Con-
trasting with her stands the gloomy figure of Hollingsworth, a
simple and uncultivated blacksmith, obsessed by a philanthropic
idea — a rather unrealistic project for the rehabilitation of
criminals. He is in need of money for the realization of his
plans, and he does not hesitate to exploit for these ends the
affection that Zenobia feels for him, but that he does not
reciprocate. To the Blithedale farm comes also Priscilla, a frail
and delicate little creature. She is a seamstress by profession
and daughter of Old Moodie, a rather decayed individual.
Priscilla attaches herself to Zenobia, but the latter's friendship
changes into jealousy when she sees that Hollingsworth is attracted by the pale charm of the little seamstress. And so
Zenobia surrenders Priscilla into the hands of Westervelt, a
mysterious person, half hypnotizer, half criminal, who has for-

merly exploited Priscilla and made her appear during his séances in the rôle of The Veiled Lady. Hollingsworth assists at such a séance, and suddenly realizing the nature of his feelings for Priscilla, he takes her away from Westervelt. Zenobia, who is really the elder sister of Priscilla — the daughter of Old Moodie in a previous and wealthier existence — disappears, exasperated by jealousy, and is later on found drowned by Foster, Hollingsworth and Coverdale.

It may seem a difficult business to introduce any Gothic romance in the description of a rural socialistic experiment in New England during the eighteen forties. The instances of such an influence are, indeed, rarer here; but still, we shall try to apply our scheme in order to find out if Hawthorne's innate predilection for reminiscences of a Gothic character nevertheless found their way into the *Blithedale Romance*.

In his introduction to the book, Hawthorne himself says that his stay at Brook Farm was "certainly the most Romantic episode of his own life," and it seems that his intention was to content himself with writing a romance of reality, without introducing any supernatural machinery. But he was unable to keep his imagination from playing with the thought of how this reality might be metamorphosed into a regular romanticised, or rather gothicized, version. When Priscilla enters the story, accompanied by Hollingsworth, Zenobia gives a mockingly scornful description of how the happenings of the evening might be turned into a ballad: "It is a grand subject, and worthy of supernatural machinery. The storm, the startling knock at the door, the entrance of the sable knight Hollingsworth and this shadowy snow-maiden, who, precisely at the stroke of midnight, shall melt away at my feet in a pool of ice-cold water and give me my death with a pair of wet slippers." This may sound like a jest, but there is something of a sinister prophecy in the facetious words: Priscilla will give Zenobia her death in ice-cold water, though she does not at the moment suspect anything of the kind. On another occasion, Zenobia is likened to a tragic actress "fumbling in her bosom for a concealed dagger or mingling the ratsbane in her lover's bowl of wine." That such a thing were impossible to imagine in New

England, but, to Hawthorne's romantic mind, a quite natural
occurence south of the Appenines, is shown by the words
which immediately follow: "And, besides, had we been in Italy,
instead of New England, it was hardly yet a crisis for the
dagger or the bowl" (5).

The mysteriousness of *A Blithedale Romance* consists chiefly
in the mesmeric faculty possessed by Priscilla and utilized by
Westervelt. We already know something of Hawthorne's attitude
towards these matters through the opinions cited from his note-
books,[1] and the same view is shown in a comment referring to
the public at the séance where Priscilla appears as the Veiled
Lady: "The epoch of rapping spirits, and all the wonders that
have followed in their trails — such as tables upset by invisible
agencies, bells self-tolled at funerals, and ghostly music per-
formed on jew's harps — had not yet arrived. And, my countrymen, methinks we have fallen on an evil age. If these phenomena have not humbug at the bottom, so much the worse for
us." Still, Hawthorne uses the effects of Westervelt's magnetism
or mesmerism much in the same way as he earlier used the
Gothic machinery. And into his description of this very modern
kind of superstition, there enters not a little of the weirdness
remembered from the Gothic Romance. Westervelt may logi-
cally be counted among the wizard types of Hawthornesque
Romance. He is a handsome man of a type decidedly Italian
or Spanish (5): "His hair, as well as his beard and mustache,
was coal-black; his eyes, too, were black and sparkling, and
his teeth remarkably brilliant." Other traits are rather to be
assigned to category (8): he has a "metallic laugh," Coverdale
says, and continues: "in the excess of his delight he opened
his mouth wide, and disclosed a gold band around the upper
part of his teeth, thereby making it apparent that every one of
his brilliant grinders and incisors was a sham. This discovery
affected me very oddly. I felt as if the whole man were a moral
and physical humbug: his wonderful beauty of face, for aught
I knew, might be removable like a mask; and, tall and comely
as his figure looked, he was perhaps but a wizened little elf,

---

[1] Cp. p. 32.

gray and decrepit, with nothing genuine about him, save the wicked expression of his grin." The artfulness of this mixture of romantic folklore and modern scientific sham is exquisite. Using the gold band round Westervelt's sham teeth as a medium, Hawthorne obtains the same effect as do the old Nordic tales of the forest witch who has no back to her lovely form.

Just as Zenobia foreshadows her own fate in the jesting words mentioned above, she tells her audience of Priscilla's peculiar nature, when she narrates the story of the silvery veil. It is, says Coverdale expressly, "undeniable nonsense," but nonsense of a very clear-sighted and not altogether kindly nature, with an undertone of menace. When finally Zenobia interrupts her tale by throwing the piece of gauze she holds in her hand, over Priscilla's head, the meaning stands quite clear to the reader: Zenobia is going to deliver the girl into Westervelt's hands. Zenobia, though in all her gorgeousness perhaps the most intense flesh-and-blood figure Hawthorne ever created, has nevertheless something magic in her being. "Zenobia is an enchantress," whispers Coverdale to Hollingsworth. " ... the flower in her hair is a talisman. If you were to snatch it away, she would vanish, or be transformed into something else."

But if Zenobia is, on the whole, a creature of earthly clay, Priscilla has all the more supernatural qualities. "Hidden things were visible to her ... and silence was audible ..." These strange faculties were explained by the modern magicians in their own way: "It was a period when science ... was bringing forward a new hoard of facts and imperfect theories, that had partially won credence in elder times, but which modern scepticism had swept away as rubbish ..." Many people had their own, strange opinions of the relations between Priscilla and her master: "Yet ... the busy tongues ... averred ... that the strange gentleman (Westervelt) was a wizard, and that he had taken advantage of Priscilla's lack of earthly substance to subject her to himself, as his familiar spirit, through whose medium he gained cognizance of whatever happened, in regions near or remote" (8).

That is the nearest Hawthorne ever comes to Gothic reminiscences in his *Blithedale Romance*. He has endeavoured and on the whole succeeded, in creating with this book a work

mainly of his own age. But, even though Zenobia lends to the
novel the whole glamour of her vivid and dynamic personality,
of all Hawthorne's novels this remains the one that makes the
faintest impression on the reader nowadays. It is possible that
Hawthorne took the same view of his own writings. In the
evolutionary curve that may be traced of the dependence on
Gothic art in Hawthorne's work, *A Blithedale Romance* stands
as the point of maximum independence between the starting-
point of recently imbibed youthful impressions and the harking
back to old sources in the works of his later years. It is possible that this development would have taken place even if
Hawthorne had stayed in America all his life. But undoubtedly
his years as Consul at Liverpool and his acquaintance with
English monuments from earlier epochs, with old legends and
with living historical tradition in Britain did much to accelerate
it. In his note-books, and in *Our Old Home* we find many
references to more or less fantastical stories that have much in
common with the Gothic tradition. During these years, however,
Hawthorne wrote no fiction in the proper sense of the word.
When he finally reverted to this field, it was under the liberating
influence of another intellectual and physical climate, during a
prolonged stay in Italy, the home of Romance, where many
half-forgotten figures and scenes from the world of the Gothic
tales rose to the surface of his mind petitioning a place in his
creations. *The Marble Faun* was regarded by Hawthorne himself as his best work, and in his Preface he states the rôle of
Italy in this "fanciful story, evolving a thoughtful moral." The
author's intention is not to portray Italian manners and the
Italian character: "Italy as the site of his Romance was chiefly
valuable to him as affording a sort of poetic or fairy precinct,
where actualities would not be so terribly insisted upon as they
are, and must needs be, in America. No author, without a
trial, can conceive of the difficulty of writing a romance about
a country where there is no shadow, no antiquity, no mystery,
no picturesque and gloomy wrong, nor anything but a common-
place prosperity, in broad and simple daylight, as is happily
the case with my dear native land... Romance and poetry, ivy,
lichens, and wall-flowers, need ruins to make them grow."

This description of the appropriate setting for a romance might have been given by Mrs. Radcliffe herself. It shows better than anything else that Hawthorne's ideal, though morally and in many respects also artistically so very superior to those of the "Gothic" authors, still had very much in common with them. We shall find further proofs of this fact by studying the composition and some details of his story of Rome: *The Marble Faun*.

The Marble Faun vies with *The Scarlet Letter* for the honour of being the most widely read of Hawthorne's romances. Apart from its literary value, it has a certain topographical interest for the tourist in Italy, and the volume is still to be found in book-shops in Rome beside Madame de Staël's *Corinne* and Zola's *Rome*.

This story traces its inception to a visit to the Capitoline Museum, where Hawthorne, who was otherwise seldom captivated by sculpture, immediately took a great interest in the so-called Faun of Praxiteles. In his Italian note-book he himself tells us of the occasion: "We afterwards went into the sculpture gallery, where I looked at the Faun of Praxiteles, and was sensible of a peculiar charm in it; a sylvan beauty and homeliness, friendly and wild at once. The lengthened but not preposterous ears, and the little tail, which we infer, have an exquisite effect, and make the spectator smile in his very heart. This race of fauns was the most delightful of all that antiquity imagined. It seems to me that a story with all sorts of fun and pathos in it, might be contrived on the idea of their species having become intermingled with the human race; a family with the faun blood in them, having prolonged itself from the classic era till our own days. The tail might have disappeared, by dint of constant intermarriages with ordinary mortals; but the pretty hairy ears should occasionally reappear in members of the family; and the moral instincts and intellectual characteristics of the faun might be most picturesquely brought out, without determent to the human interest of the story."[1]

Such a figure was just what Hawthorne needed to illustrate

---

[1] *Hawthorne's Italian Note-book*, April 22nd, 1858.

his now yet further developed theory about the rôle of sin in man's mental and intellectual development. Donatello, the chief personage of the story, is a scion of just such an old Italian family as was described in the note-book. He is beautiful, healthy and gay, an unsophisticated child of nature without any consciousness of sin but also without any higher development of character. At Rome, he makes the acquaintance of a coterie of young artists and falls in love with the beautiful and mysterious Miriam, a lady of unknown origin whose past life remains a riddle to the reader throughout the book. Some sort of connection with Miriam's past is, however, traceable in a model, a sort of demoniacal lazzarone, who follows everywhere in her wake. One evening, he appears when Miriam and Donatello are standing just at the edge of the Tarpeian precipice, and, in a fit of passion, Donatello seizes the man and holds him above the abyss. With a glance, he consults Miriam, before he lets him fall to be crushed against the stones at the foot of the rock. Thus Donatello has come to know sin and is going to be familiar with the sense of guilt — a guilt that he shares with Miriam, because it is she who has given him the final sanction for accomplishing the deed. A shadow of guilt also falls on Hilda, Miriam's friend, a young girl who is a perfect specimen of the idealized "American womanhood" that Hawthorne often praises. She is beautiful, pious and pure of heart. Each day, when she has finished her work, which consists in copying the works of the old masters, she returns to her attic, in front of which she keeps alive the lamp before an image of the Virgin Mary, and feeds white doves that assemble there. The continuation of the story is enacted partly in Rome, partly on Donatello's family estate in the vicinity of Florence. It is a description of how Donatello and Miriam, like two damned spirits, roam about separated, in quest of a peace which neither of them shall ever be able to find. Donatello is no longer in possession of the mysterious contact with nature that has formerly been his greatest joy as well as the most salient feature of his character. Miriam cannot free herself from her gloomy mood, even though she has been delivered of her persecutor. At last they meet at Perugia, and after having spent some time together at Rome during the carnival, they part for ever. Donatello gives himself up to justice in order to expiate his crime. The fate of Miriam remains unknown to the reader. Hilda, who has also made a confession — in spite of her Protestantic faith uttered in a whisper in a confessional at St. Peter's, achieves peace after an inner struggle, and finally marries Kenyon, the fourth member of the set.

Here, we are not concerned with the personal development of these three personages. The substance of Hawthorne's message in this book seems to me to be expressed in the following words, uttered by Kenyon on the last page of the work: "Sin has educated Donatello, and elevated him. Is sin then — which we deem such a dreadful blackness to the universe — is it, like sorrow, merely an element of human education, through which we struggle to a higher and purer state than we should otherwise have attained? Did Adam fall that we might ultimately rise to a far loftier paradise than his?" In *The Marble Faun*, Hawthorne has, on the whole, better than anywhere else succeeded in his endeavour to instil something of real human life into the bearers of his ideas. We watch Donatello's development from a pagan and carefree youth, full of animal spirits, into a grown-up man with a deep sense of responsibility who uprightly and consciously aspires towards righteous life. His confession is not the result of external pressure, like Dimmesdale's, but the outcome of a free inner development — a transformation.

The Gothic trick of presenting the story as if found in an old manuscript has here been discarded by Hawthorne. But otherwise, it is rather amazing how many of the old patterns appear when he proceeds to write a romantic story from the enchanted country of Romance. He tells it, of course, in his usual, rather sceptical way; but, to a higher degree than elsewhere, it is felt that he assumes the reader to be inspired by a romantic feeling which makes all sorts of supernatural and wonderful things quite plausible. Proceeding with our tabulation, we now arrive at item (2), the Gothic castle, and we soon recognize it without any difficulty, standing in the Florentine landscape and free of all disguise.

The title that Hawthorne first gave to his novel was *The Romance of Monte Beni*, and it was under this name that the book was first printed in America. Monte Beni is the ancestral castle of Donatello — for which the Villa Montauto near Florence, where Hawthorne had been staying some time in 1858, was the model — and the description of the building leaves little to be desired as to age, loneliness and other traditional attributes of the Gothic castle. It possesses ancient battlements and an "owl tower" with a prisoner's cell, where in olden days a necromancer was kept prisoner. It is now converted into a chapel, with a crucifix, a Bambino and a human skull carved in alabaster as chief adornments. The castle also contains a big entrance room, which Hawthorne likens to an "Etruscan tomb," and "an almost interminable vista of apartments . . . reminding him (Kenyon) of the hundred rooms in Blue Beard's castle, or the countless halls in some palace of the Arabian nights."

Still more weirdly Gothic is the description of the catacombs of St. Calixtus, where Miriam has a mysterious and frightening interview with her strange and awe-inspiring follower. Comparison made on the spot shows that the description is strictly accurate. These ancient subterranean passages certainly do possess an atmosphere of dark mystery, corresponding fairly exactly to Hawthorne's conception of the ideal surroundings for a ghostly interview. To him they must have been a great find — the very scenes of the beloved books of his boyhood come true. Conscientiously he records the itinerary for the tourists: "Sometimes their gloomy pathway tended upward, so that, through a crevice, a little daylight glimmered down upon them, or even a streak of sunshine peeped into a burial niche; then again they went downward by gradual descent, or by abrupt, rudely hewn steps, into deeper and deeper recesses of the earth . . ." Further on, "they found two sarcophagi, one containing a skeleton, and the other a shrivelled body, which still wore the garments of its former lifetime." Reality such as this more than equals the most terrific descriptions of subterranean cellars belonging to Italian convents or Spanish castles to be met with in the original Gothic novels.

Passing on to item (3) on our list, we find the mysterious

crime as the chief secret of Miriam's dark destiny. The connection between her and the model, who is later found to be a Capuchin friar, is never made quite clear, but Hawthorne hints several times at a parallelism between Miriam's fate and that of Beatrice Cenci, whose portrait is copied by Hilda. Here we thus find the religious character of the crime, which is also possibly of incestuous nature[1] — the very model of the crimes of Gothic romance. The second crime in the novel — the murder of the model by Donatello — is of a different kind, chiefly meant to illustrate Hawthorne's idea of sin and its consequences.

Number (4) is represented, as has already been pointed out, by the model, who is found to be a Capuchin monk. Here we shall linger for a moment to look at the event which forms the climax of the action: the death of the model. The beggar — who is really a monk — is hurled down the Tarpeian rock and crushed at its foot. The fall is not described from a visual point of view. As often elsewhere,[2] Hawthorne contents himself with giving the auditive effects: "Along with it (the struggle) was a loud, fearful cry, which quivered upward through the air, and sank quivering downward to the earth. Then, a silence." But we hardly err, if we see in this downfall a reminiscence of Lewis's monk when he is precipitated down a rock by the devil, or of Melmoth, whose fall is so obviously copied in Hawthorne's first literary attempt *Fanshawe*. These men, who are hurled down craggy precipices, appear abundantly throughout Romantic literature. The real Count Victorin tumbles down a steep rock before Medardus assumes his rôle,[3] and a little later Claude Frollo falls headlong from the towers of Notre Dame.[4] It is tempting to try to picture the immediate reaction of Hawthorne when he stood for the first time on the edge of the Tarpeian Rock. He described the occasion in his Italian notebook.[5] He and his wife had been to tea with Fredrika Bremer,

---

[1] Beatrice Cenci was, according to the legend, violated by her father.
[2] Cp. *The Hollow of the Three Hills*, p. 35 of the present essay.
[3] E. T. A. Hoffmann, *Die Elixiere des Teufels*.
[4] Victor Hugo, *Notre Dame de Paris*. Cp. Killen, *Le roman terrifiant*, p. 183.
[5] May 22nd, 1858.

who was at the time staying in Rome, and afterwards the
party went out to look at the precipice. The note-book contains
no reference to any future literary application of the motive.
Hawthorne only notes that he has seen "the famous precipice,
down which the old Romans used to fling their traitors, or
sometimes, indeed, their patriots," but perhaps just at that
moment, before the dispassionate gaze of the unsuspecting little
Swedish lady, was born the strange hybrid between a satyr, a
ghost, and a monk, which in Hawthorne's last great romance,
was to find his death at the foot of the Tarpeian Rock. Other
passages relating to the Roman Church are not of any immediate
interest for the theme analyzed in this essay.

The rôle of Italy in the story is clearly that of presenting
the action under a more romantic aspect as taking place beneath
the sky of southern Europe and among historical ruins and
antiquities of different kinds. But, to Hawthorne, Italy is not
only a storehouse of antiquities. It is also the centre of the
Old World, filled with memories of hoary crimes and iniquity.
We recall his words about its value as a setting cited from the
Preface of the book.[1] Speaking of the Villa Borghese, he once
says: "Just an instant before it was Arcadia and the Golden
Age. The spell being broken, it was now only that old tract
of pleasure-ground close by the people's gate of Rome — a
tract where the crimes and calamities of ages, the many battles,
blood recklessly poured out, and deaths of myriads, have
corrupted all the soil, creating an influence that makes the air
deadly to human lungs." This impression of Rome as something
positively corrupted goes through the whole narrative, culminat-
ing in a passage likening the Eternal City to a "long-decaying
corpse,"[2] an uncomfortable and inhospitable-seeming abode to
a citizen of the New World, but still possessing its own inimit-
able fascination.

The spectres (7) of the Gothic novel are also embodied in
the person of Miriam's model. Another instance, showing
Hawthorne's trust in his readers' readiness when it comes to
accepting ghost-like effects, is given in the description of the

[1] Cp. above p. 74.
[2] *The Marble Faun*, Chapter XXXVI, *Hilda's Tower*.

nightly visit paid by a company of tourists to the Coliseum. Here the sculptor Kenyon acts as the author's mouthpiece when he says: "Fancy a nightly assemblage of eighty thousand melancholy and remorseful ghosts, looking down from those tiers of broken arches, striving to repent of the savage pleasures which they once enjoyed, but still longing to enjoy them over again." Whereupon Hilda rejoins: "You bring a Gothic horror into this peaceful moonlight scene." A few moments afterwards, the real spectre, the model, makes his appearance. The character of this very compound figure is certainly partly spectral (7), but it is perhaps still more that of a sorcerer (8): Miriam appears to be a bewitched person, as soon as he approaches. When catching sight of him, "fancying herself wholly unseen, the beautiful Miriam began to gesticulate extravagantly, gnashing her teeth, flinging her arms wildly abroad, stamping with her feet. It was as if she had stepped aside for an instant, solely to snatch the relief of a brief fit of madness." Even though Hawthorne gives a sort of psychological explanation of her demeanour, stating that she wished to "relieve her nerves in this wild way," the similarity between her gestures and the traditional witch dances is nevertheless striking. Elsewhere, too, Miriam is depicted as a woman with a bent towards the supernatural: "She has . . . a suggestive power, a magnetic influence, a sympathetic knowledge."

The model is, indeed, a strange mixture of different romantic types. In the chapter entitled "The Spectre of the Catacombs," he is mentioned as an artist's model "of exceedingly picturesque and even melodramatic aspect." His costume is that of a Roman peasant, but under his broad-brimmed hat "a wild visage was indistinctly seen, floating away, as it were, into a dusky wilderness of mustache and beard. His eyes winked, and turned uneasily from the torches, like a creature to whom midnight would be more congenial than noonday." When he speaks, his voice is hoarse and harsh: "Inquire not what I am, nor wherefore I abide in the darkness," he says, " . . . She (Miriam) has called me forth, and must abide the consequence of my reappearance in the world." And so begins his sinister influence "such as beasts and reptiles of subtle and evil nature sometimes exercise upon their victims ... That iron chain ... must have been forged in some such unhallowed furnace as is only kindled by evil passions and fed by evil deeds." We might here point to item (8) in our tabulation, the Italian villain in pact with the Devil, as well as to (7), spectres, and (8), magicians. Hawthorne has used all the resources of Gothic machinery to suggest the same impression of fright as the old novels of terror had once awakened. At the same time, his use of them is as sceptically circumspect as possible, taking care not to run the risk of an accusation that he belonged to the Gothic school himself. To a modern reader, the attraction of these Gothic mysteries remains incomprehensible, but that the flavour bestowed was heartily relished by contemporary readers is shown by a letter to the author from Motley, cited by Lathrop in an introductory note to *The Marble Faun:*[1] "I like those shadowy, weird, fantastic Hawthornesque shapes flitting through the golden gloom which is the atmosphere of the book. I like the misty way in which the story is indicated rather than revealed."

An equivalent to the magic potions of the sorcerers (8) is also described in the novel. In the grounds around Donatello's ancestral castle, the peasants cultivate and press a wine, the manufacture of which has from time immemorial been a family secret. The wine is called Sunshine, and it possesses "hidden peculiarities and subtile exquisiteness;" the drinking of it is "more a moral than a physical enjoyment." But all these properties would — just as is really the case with so many excellent Italian wines — vanish and evaporate if it were sent to the market, i. e. transported some distance. Once more, Hawthorne has found the wonderful in a quite ordinary fact.

The magic of the fine arts (11) also plays a rôle in this book, in which Hawthorne has definitively stated his opinion of imitative art on the whole. He had no very great comprehension of it; sculptured figures in the nude seemed to him as unnatural as indecent, and the picture galleries wearied him. It is rather characteristic that the painter who found most favour in the sight of Hawthorne was Guido Reni with his sugary sweetness: two of the works of this artist play a certain rôle

---

[1] Riverside Edition.

in the action of the novel. One of them is the picture of the Archangel Gabriel putting his foot on the monster of evil, hung in the Capuchin monastery — the significance of this picture chiefly belongs to the discussion of certain ethical problems in the book, but some importance may be ascribed to the fact that the demon, on which the Archangel is setting his foot and which is commonly reputed to ressemble Cardinal Pamfili, is found to bear a striking likeness to Miriam's model. The fact is acknowledged both by Kenyon and by Hilda "and it added not a little to the grotesque and weird character which, half playfully, half seriously, they assigned to Miriam's attendant, to think of him as personating the demon's part in a picture of more than two centuries ago." The second picture is the portrait of Beatrice Cenci, which is connected in some way or other with Miriam's destiny. During a conversation between Miriam and Hilda, who has copied the portrait, a faint light is thrown over Miriam's mystery: "It was," says Hawthorne, "a sorrow that removed this beautiful girl out of the sphere of humanity, and set her in a far-off region, the remoteness of which — while yet her face is so close before us — makes us shiver as at a spectre." Hilda considers Beatrice sinless, but Miriam asserts that "Beatrice's own conscience does not acquit her of something evil, and never to be forgiven . . . It was a terrible guilt, an inexpiable crime, and she feels it to be so." It is in this way that Hawthorne suggests the real nature of Miriam's mysterious past (3) and explains the sadness that surrounds her.

But the magic of art is not inherent only in pictures. We have seen that Hawthorne got the inspiration for his book while admiring the Faun of Praxiteles, and the inward and outward resemblance between the statue and Donatello is stressed throughout the story. Many readers have complained that they never got to know whether Donatello's ears were pointed and hairy like those of the real faun — not as many have expressed their curiosity as to the little tail. These are secrets that Hawthorne has taken with him in his grave, leaving the problem, with an amused smile, to be conned by people whose imagination is not of his own lofty kind. But in the story we find also other sculptures, more or less akin to the wandering statues of Gothic romance. Kenyon, when staying at Monte Beni, models a bust of Donatello. During his work, "Kenyon gave up all preconceptions about the character of his subject, and let his hands work uncontrolled with the clay, somewhat as a spiritual medium, while holding a pen, yields it to an unseen guidance other than that of her own will." It is just at the time when Donatello undergoes his transformation, and the bust, after having first shown a beautifully spiritual expression, is changed, by some accidental handling of the clay by the sculptor, so as to show "a distorted and violent look, combining animal fierceness with intelligent hatred." Had Hilda or Miriam seen the bust, says Hawthorne, they might have recognized Donatello's face as it was when he flung the model down the Tarpeian precipice. But the final result is different: "It gives," says Hilda of the sculpture, when it is later on shown to her, "the impression of a growing intellectual power and moral sense . . . it is the Faun, but advancing towards a state of higher development." Thus, the bust of Donatello shows his spiritual development in a way not altogether different from the way in which the prophetic pictures reflected the evolution of the destinies of young Walter Ludlow and his wife.[1]

When Donatello and Miriam are united for the first time after the period of purification, they meet alone by the statue of Pope Julius III at Perugia. They soon separate again, in order to proceed on their ways to Rome, and in that moment, "Miriam, Donatello, and the sculptor, all three imagined that they beheld the bronze pontiff endowed with spiritual life. A blessing was felt descending upon them from his outstretched hand." The description may be understood as an interpretation of the power inherent in every great work of art. Perhaps there is also contained in it some reminiscences of the sort of mysteries included under (11) in our scheme.

When Miriam and Donatello have perpetrated their crime, they feel that they have been united by a new, strange bond. The life of the model has strung them together for all times to come, their affinity is, as Donatello expresses himself, "for ever-

[1] Cp. pp. 41—43 of the present essay.

more cemented with his blood." Saying this, Donatello starts, and tells himself that it is "cemented with blood, which would corrupt and grow more noisome forever and forever, but bind them none the less strictly for that." The truth of the uniting power of a crime perpetrated in common has here found an expression founded on the traditions of Gothic romance and the strange faculties ascribed to blood that had been admitted into the general consciousness (12). Another and far more conspicuous specimen of "Gothic" blood is met with in the scene where the dead monk — or model — is lying on his *lit de parade* in the church of the Capuchin monastery. "As the three friends stood by the bier, they saw that a little stream of blood had begun to ooze from the dead monk's nostrils: it crept slowly towards the thicket of his beard, where, in the course of a moment or two, it hid itself." The obvious inference is immediately drawn by the sin-oppressed Miriam: "How can we tell but that the murderer of this monk may have just entered the church?" she asks. This is one of the passages which make it impossible for the present-day reader to take this book quite seriously, though in many respects it is so surprisingly up-to-date. The familiar and current superstition that Hawthorne here treats as a matter of course has, in the course of the intervening century, become an antiquated and ridiculous conception.

As has been shown by the above analysis, Hawthorne has introduced a great number of recollections from the world of Gothic romance into this novel of 1859. In subsequent products from his pen, he was to continue his experiments with this machinery and move still further away from the firm ground of reality. At his death, he left four unfinished manuscripts, all of them dealing with two themes. One was the vivifying elixir of youth, which had long been occupying his imagination. The other motive had presented itself to him on a visit to Smithell's Hall, an English manor-house. There, a footprint on a flagstone was shown to him, that was said to have been left by the bloody foot of a murderer. At Hawthorne's visit to the place, his hostess asked him to "write a ghost-story for her house," and in his note-book he jotted down that the legend was "a good one."[1] The first sketch of a romance located to England and treating this theme is *The Ancestral Footstep*, of which a couple of notes, arranged in the form of a diary, have been published after the author's death. He then abandoned the theme of the bloody imprint for a time, writing *The Marble Faun* and *Dr. Grimshawe's Secret* and editing his English note-books. Afterwards, he reverted to it in the unfinished novel called *Septimius Felton*, and finally he once more began to rewrite the story. Of this last version only three chapters exist and have been published under the name of *The Dolliver Romance*. The theme of the Elixir of life occurs in *Septimius Felton* and *The Dolliver Romance*. These unfinished novels will here be treated in their chronological order.

Already in 1886, the German scholar Anton Schönbach made the four manuscripts the subject of a careful analysis;[2] starting from an investigation of Hawthorne's note-books and manuscripts, he first examined his working method, and then proceeded to disentangle other problems such as the influence of German literature, and especially of Tieck,[2] on Hawthorne's productions. Schönbach's work is highly appreciated by later students of Hawthorne, and in the following I shall avail myself of his results as to dates and certain other facts.

The Ancestral Footstep is nothing more than a preparatory sketch. In 1858, Hawthorne drew these outlines of the English Romance that had haunted his mind ever since his visit to Smithell's Hall. Strangely enough, the English family legend has traits in common with an idea jotted down in his notebook five years before his visit to England:[3] "The print in blood of a naked foot to be traced through the street of a town." The outlines of the story are written in the form of a diary and give a disconnected, sometimes contradictory summary of the projected tale. The final version is as follows: Middleton is the descendant of a family that has long been resident in America. His ancestor had left England after a bitter dissension with a brother of his. Both brothers had loved the same girl,

---

[1] *Hawthorne's English Note-book*, August 25th. 1855.
[2] Anton Schönbach, *Beiträge zur Charakteristik Nathaniel Hawthornes. Anglia*, 1886. Cp. p. 13 & 28 above.
[3] *Hawthorne's American Note-book*, December 19th, 1850.

and she had been prevailed upon to marry the elder one. On the wedding-day, however, the bride and the younger brother both disappeared. The elder brother never married and left his title and estate to a third brother who had been wounded in a quarrel between the brothers before the flight. He had then left a bloody trace on the stone steps in front of the house.

Middleton has some old family documents in his possession and takes them with him to England, where he meets an old man, inmate of a Hospital. The estate is now owned by a Mr. Eldredge, who "shall have an Italian mother and shall have the personal characteristics of an Italian." "Dark suspicion of past crime, and of the possibility of future crime, may be thrown around him." Middleton, who has in the meantime been appointed American minister to one of the minor Continental courts, is invited to spend some days at the castle. There he opens an old cupboard, to which he has brought the ancestral key, and finds some old documents. Eldredge tries to murder Middleton by offering him a goblet of poisoned wine — a repetition of a crime perpetrated two hundred years earlier — but does not succeed. Middleton marries Alice, niece of the aged inmate of the hospital.

This short summary only gives the chief outlines of the action, which is changed during the course of the work. Hawthorne had originally meant to have the story told by a gentleman whom he had first met during his years as Consul at Liverpool. Thus, the introduction would have assumed something of the same character as the famous prefatory sketch to *The Scarlet Letter*, with its description of his life as a customs officer at Salem.

In this rough draught for another great romance, we recognize, to begin with, the artifice of telling the story from another person's point of view (1), and further the castle (2), the Italian villain (5), and the bloody imprint (12). It would seem that Hawthorne met with certain difficulties in the further development of the intrigue and therefore abandoned the manuscript while busying himself with other tasks. During one of the following years, he composed his next story, which we possess in the form of an undated manuscript edited by his son, Julian Hawthorne, under the title of *Dr. Grimshawe's Secret.*

Dr. Grimshawe is "an elderly person of grim aspect," who lives about the beginning of the 19th century in a small New England town together with two adopted children, Ned and Elsie. The house, which stands on the outskirts of a graveyard, is of a strange appearance, especially Dr. Grimshawe's study is "overlaid with dust, that in lack of a visiting card, you might write your name with your forefinger upon the tables; and so hung with cobwebs, that they assumed the appearance of dusky upholstery." The Doctor has a quaint predilection for spiders, of which he possesses many varieties, but, in particular, one huge specimen. The Doctor tells the children legends of olden times in England; there often recurs a story about a family, one member of which had assisted at the beheading of King Charles I, and therefore always afterwards left a bloody track behind him wherever he went. He was imprisoned in his ancestral castle, but escaped, and finally came over to New England.

The old Doctor is a very unpopular man, and is once assailed by a mob in the street. He is saved by a delicate-looking stranger, Colcord, who afterwards comes to live in the Doctor's house for some time. Colcord is a schoolmaster, and the descendant of an old English family. One night he mysteriously disappears. Some time afterwards Grimshawe dies. Ned preserves some old documents of which the Doctor has often spoken.

Many years later, a stranger named Redclyffe comes to England. He meets an old man who turns out to be none other than Colcord. Redclyffe is the boy Ned, now a grown-up man and a successful American civil servant. The master of a neighbouring castle, Braithwaite, is half Italian. He and Redclyffe, who has in the meantime been appointed American Minister to a European court, meet at a dinner in the Hospital, and Redclyffe is invited to the castle. There, he finds a Jesuit priest, who shows him the library, where are to be found not only a book-worm but also a huge spider of the kind that Dr Grimshawe cherished. Later on, Braithwaite offers him a strange wine. Redclyffe faints away and awakes in a closed chamber. Opposite him sits a strange figure, and he remembers the family legend told him by Dr Grimshawe, about "the undying one" of the manor-house, a former Edward Redclyffe who had been treacherously imprisoned. When he speaks to the figure, it sinks down in a rattling heap on the floor, "as if a thing of dry bones had been suddenly loosened at the joints." Colcord and the warden of the hospital go to the castle to ask for Redclyffe, but are told that he has already left. This Colcord refuses to believe. "Dark, murderous man," says he to Braithwa te, "your course has not been unwatched; the secrets of this mansion are not unknown. For two centuries back, they have been better known to them who dwell afar off than to those resident within the mansion. The foot that made the Bloody Footstep has returned from its long wanderings, and it passes on straight as destiny — sure as an avenging Providence — to the punishment and destruction of those who incur retribution." Saying this, Colcord advances through a previously unseen door in the panels of the wall, into a narrow, dark passage. He opens a segment of the floor, which gives access to a flight of small, dark stairs. Followed by the other members of the party, he arrives in a gloomy cell where they find Redclyffe and an old coffer to which Redclyffe has the key, given him once by Dr Grimshawe. When the coffer is opened, it is found to contain "golden ringlets, abundant, clustering through the whole coffer, and living with elasticity." These are the only remains of the whole bodily substance of a legendary person, known as the Beauty of the Golden Locks. Colcord possesses such a lock, and thus can show himself to be the rightful heir of the mansion. Redclyffe has been educated by Dr Grimshawe, who hated the old family, in order to enable the doctor to impose a foundling on them.

The plot of this story is much better worked out than that of *The Ancestral Footstep*, though several inconsistencies also occur in this narrative. Here, we shall only trace the principal features of the work and its connection with the tradition of Gothic Romance. We thus find the old castle (1) with its secret passages and even a family ghost (7), the dark crimes, both that of a bygone generation and that of the present owner of the mansion (2). There is an Italian priest in the castle, a person possessing "a mildness, gentleness, softness, and asking-of-leave,

in his manner, which he (Redclyffe) had not observed in persons
so well assured of their position as the Church of England
clergy" (3). Braithwaite is partly of Italian birth: "There have
been three descents of this man's branch in Italy," says the
warden of the Hospital, "and only one English mother in all
that time."

"His civility is Italian, such as oftentimes among his countrymen has offered a cup of poison to a guest, or insinuated the
stab of a stiletto into his heart" (5). Dr. Grimshawe has many
traits in common with the magicians of the novels of terror and
wonder (8). A speciality of his is his collection of spiders, which
we have met before in Hawthorne's productions as symbols of
mystery and evil thoughts.[1] The graveyard outside the Doctor's
house contains some specimens of common English garden
flowers "which could not be accounted for, — unless, perhaps,
they had sprung from some English maiden's heart, where the
intense love of those homely things, and regret of them in the
foreign land, had conspired together to keep their vivifying
principle, and cause its growth after the poor girl was buried."[2]
But otherwise this cemetery has little in common with item (7)
in our schedule: "So far as ever came to the present writer's
knowledge, there was no whisper of Doctor Grimshawe's house
being haunted; a fact on which both writer and reader may
congratulate themselves, the ghostly chord having been played
upon in these days until it has become wearisome and nauseous
as the familiar tune of a barrel-organ." The poisoned drink
which Braithwaite offers Redclyffe is, on the other hand, an
undisguised loan from the novels of terror (8), and likewise the
legend of the bloody footstep (12). Inserted in the story is also
a mysterious tale of Ormskirk, a man in a lonely chamber,
which is equipped with all the paraphernalia of Gothic Romance:
"What is the furniture? An antique chair, — one chair, no
more. A table, many-footed, of dark wood; it holds writing-
materials, a book, too, on its face, with the dust gathered on
its back. There is, moreover, a sort of antique box, or coffer,
of some dark wood, that seems to have been wrought or carved

---

[1] Cp. p. 43, *Dr. Heidegger's Experiment.*
[2] Cp. pp. 60, 93.

with skill, wondrous skill, of some period when the art of carving wainscot arms and devices was much practised; so that on this coffer — you see faces in relief of knight and dame, lords, heraldic animals; some story, very likely, told, almost revelling in Gothic sculpture of wood, like what we have seen on the marble sarcophagus of the old Greeks. It has, too, a lock, elaborately ornamented and inlaid with silver.

"What else; only spider's webs spinning strangely over everything; over that light which comes into the room through the stone; over everything. And now we see, in a corner, a strange great spider curiously variegated. The ugly, terrible, seemingly poisonous thing makes us shudder.

"What else: There are pistols; they lie on the coffer: There is a curiously shaped Italian dagger, of the kind which in a groove has poison that makes its wound mortal. On the old mantel-piece, over the fireplace, there is a vial in which are kept certain poisons."

Here, Hawthorne has heaped more relics from the Gothic store-rooms of his mind than perhaps ever before. The accumulation may have been caused by the influence of the ancient buildings seen in England and the old traditions told him there. It may also have been the natural development of his own brooding fantasy, or a combination of both. We find the same tendency in the two later manuscripts.

Septimius Felton, which was written in 1861 and later on edited by Hawthorne's daughter Una in collaboration with Robert Browning, is subtitled "The Elixir of Life." Septimius Felton, a young student of theology with an Indian strain in him, is first introduced during a conversation with two of his friends, Rose Garfield and Robert Hagburn, in the course of which he expresses his opinion that human life is too short: "so much preparation to live, and then no life at all: a ponderous beginning and nothing more." He wants an illimited space of time. Some time afterwards, the British soldiers of Boston go out to quench the revolutionary elements. Septimius takes up his gun and is challenged by a young British officer, whom he kills. Before dying the officer, who belongs to a very old English family, the Nortons, gives him a miniature, pierced by

a shot, his watch, a silver key and an old document. According to the wish of the deceased, Septimius buries him on the spot where he has died. The picture is sent to a specified address in England. Septimius occupies himself with the deciphering of the document, which is unintelligible to him. In a few months there arrives from England a pale girl, Sybil Dacy, who becomes a friend of Rose's and is often seen in the vicinity of the British soldier's unknown grave. Dr. Portsoaken, who has formerly been military doctor, tells Septimius of a lost recipe for an elixir of life. He also studies spiders — every thread of a spider's web is to him "more worth than a thread of gold" — and hints something about the interesting family history of the dead British officer. Dr. Portsoaken is also very interested in a recipe possessed by Septimius' old, hag-like, half Indian Aunt Keziah, of which the story goes that "it was the very drink which used to be passed round at witch-meetings, being brewed from the Devil's own recipe." The description is really inherited from an old Indian sachem, and it lacks only one ingredient to become a veritable elixir of life. The doctor now tells Septimius that the very document in his possession is an old recipe of such an elixir, a concoction made by Friar Bacon, and upon closer examination, it turns out to be the very same description as Aunt Keziah's, containing one more ingredient, the wonderful herb Sanguinea sanguinissima. Sybil Dacy also tells of a man who needed for manufacturing this same drink the blood of an innocent maiden. Having slain her, he always left a bloody track behind him which remained for ever engraved on the steps in front of his family mansion.

Septimius, who has found out from the old document that the maker of the elixir must lead a completely passionless life — an opportunity for Hawthorne to criticise Emerson's theories of self-culture — renounces from his love, and Rose marries Hagburn. Portsoaken tells Septimius that a member of the Norton family emigrated to America many centuries ago and there married an Indian girl; their son was the sachem from whom Keziah has inherited her recipe, and Septimius is thus partly a descendant of the same family as the man he has killed. Septimius decides to try to prepare the concoction and plucks a flower that grows on Norton's grave, believing it to be the Sanguinea sanguinissima. He wants to share his discovery with Sybil. She drinks the elixir, and then crushes the glass and dies. It is now explained that Sybil was formerly the fiancée of Norton. At first she had come to avenge herself on Septimius, but had instead fallen in love with him, and now she has saved his life. Septimius departs for England in quest of his ancestral home.

The fantastic story outlined here includes, as we have seen, a fairly complete set of Gothic paraphernalia. The central feature, the Elixir of life (8), we have already met with in the short stories of Hawthorne.[1] An old document plays a very important part (1), and the family castle is there, though only in the distance. The flower on a grave belongs under (7) of our list. We may recall that Chillingworth looked for the ingredients of his concoctions among the graves, and that the English flowers on the churchyard outside Dr. Grimshawe's house were supposed to grow out of a young maiden's heart.[2] Old Aunt Keziah, who is described as "as strange a mixture of an Indian squaw and herb doctress, with the crabbed old maid, and a mingling of the witch-aspect running through all, as could well be imagined," comes under (8). Dr. Portsoaken has also something of an old wizard in him, and the spiders, which we recently met in Dr. Grimshawe's study, are familiar to us as belonging to the equipment of Hawthorne's sorcerers. The bloody footstep (12), finally, is to be traced throughout the family story of the Nortons. The legend of Friar Bacon's drink, in which the heart's blood of a pure girl was the chief ingredient (12), is also of a sufficiently sinister character to be termed Gothic.

Once more, Hawthorne tried to use the theme of the elixir of life. *The Dolliver Romance* is only a short fragment of three scenes. The first of them describes the life of the old apothecary, Mr. Dolliver, and his little great-grandchild Pansie. The Doctor is bent and silverhaired, but keeps in good vigour thanks to a medicine concocted by his late grandson. The second scene depicts how the work on the composition of this

---

[1] Cp. p. 43, *Dr. Heidegger's Experiment.*
[2] Cp. pp. 60 and 90.

medicine, that was to have been a veritable elixir of life, ended
in the death of the man who undertook it. One morning, when
Dr. Dolliver is working in the garden with little Pansie, she
finds an herb which is afterwards thrown into a grave, soon
filled. Dr. Dolliver remembers how his wife during the summer
previous to her death used to wear this kind of flowers "day
after day, through the whole season of their bloom, in her
bosom, where they glowed like a gem, and deepened her
somewhat pallid beauty with a richness never before seen in it."
The third fragment shows an old colonel, who has noticed that
the apothecary is getting younger instead of older, coming to
visit Mr. Dolliver. He talks about a Bloody Footstep, "bearing
its track through his race," and about a mysterious stranger,
who has once given the apothecary a "musty bit of parchment,
on which were written some words, hardly legible, in an antique
hand." The apothecary had tried to concoct the medicine
described, and the stranger had finally returned and mixed a
powder into the drink, whereupon he disappeared. This potation is, according to the colonel, his hereditary property, and
he now demands it back. The apothecary tries to dissuade
him on account of the danger of drinking more than one drop
a day. But the colonel gives him a purse full of gold and
finally points his revolver at him. When he gets the flask, he
quaffs great draughts, and the effect is terrifying: "The Colonel
sat a moment in his chair, panting for breath; then started to
his feet with a prompt vigor that contrasted widely with the
infirm and rheumatic movements that had heretofore characterized him. He struck his forehead violently with one hand, and
smote his chest with the other: he stamped his foot thunderously
on the ground; then he leaped up to the ceiling, and came
down with an elastic bound. Then he laughed, a wild, exulting
haha with a strange triumphant roar that filled the house and
reechoed through it; a sound full of fierce, animal rapture —
enjoyment of sensual life mixed up with a sort of horror."
Soon he falls down dead. His countenance is in the first instant a young man's, and in the next moment it is grown
"ashen, withered, shrunken, more aged than in life."
    In this fragment we encounter again several of the themes

cherished by Hawthorne from the years when he wrote his short stories. There is the elixir (8) from *Dr. Heidegger's Experiment* and *Septimius Felton*, the recipe of which is written on a scroll of parchment (1). There is the mysterious exotic flower, which we first met in the story of *Rappacini's Daughter* (8), and the bloody footstep (12) that stalks through all Hawthorne's later works. There is little indication as to which was the central idea in this last work of Hawthorne's. But the short scenes we possess of this romance show him at his best as a stylist. The description of the life of Mr. Dolliver and little Pansie is a delightful idyll, and the painting of Mr. Dolliver's vigil is a good psychological study of an ageing man's reactions: "And thus it happened with poor Grandsir Dolliver, who often awoke from an old man's fitful sleep with a sense that his senile predicament was but a dream of the past night; and hobbling hastily across the cold floor to the looking-glass, he would be grievously disappointed at beholding his white hair, the wrinkles and furrows, the ashen visage and bent form, the melancholy mask of age, in which, as he now remembered, some strange and sad enchantment had involved him for years gone by." As in the story of *Dr. Heidegger's Experiment*, the powerlessness of man against decay and death is here put before us. The end of the experiment is not so tragic in the short story, where Hawthorne makes the four enchanted persons revert to the customary tenor of old age. But Sybil Dacy (in *Septimius Felton*) has to forfeit her life for trying the powerful potation, and so has the colonel of the present fragment. The tools of the Gothic romancers have here, as elsewhere in Hawthorne's works, been used to impress a stern and implacable psychological truth.

*   *   *

Here our investigation of the influence of Gothic Romance on Nathaniel Hawthorne's work has come to an end. It is to be hoped that the facts adduced justify the view that Gothic Romance formed an important substratum of Hawthorne's productions — perhaps not always consciously used, but ever present and often employed for definite artistic purposes. It would be unjust to stamp him as a surviving Goth. His artistic ambition places him on a much higher level than the European authors that are generally referred to as "Gothic." He belongs to the same generation and class of literary artists as Edgar Allan Poe or E. T. A. Hoffmann. But in him, the properties that are usually comprised under the term Puritan formed a strange and strong counterweight to his bent for the fantastical, and it is in the mingling and interaction of such influences from many quarters, but chiefly of these two currents, that Hawthorne's genius is to be sought and found. The amalgamation was made with great conscious artistry and followed carefully prepared lines. As we have seen, Hawthorne's use of the Gothic elements was comparatively profuse in his first short stories; it waned during the middle period of his productions, to be revived in his latest works.

BIBLIOGRAPHY

Hawthorne's Works:

The Works of Nathaniel Hawthorne, with introductory notes by George Parsons Lathrop. Riverside Edition. Boston & New York 1890. 13 vols.

The Works of Nathaniel Hawthorne, with introductions by Katherine Lee Bates. New York, 1902. 7 vols.

Hawthorne's First Diary edited by T. Pickard. London, 1897.

The American Note-books by Nathaniel Hawthorne. Based upon the manuscripts in the Pierpont Morgan Library and edited by Randall Stewart. Yale University Press, New Haven, 1902.

Other Works of Fiction:

E. Spenser, *The Faerie Queene*.

J. Milton, *Paradise Lost*.

J. Bunyan, *Pilgrim's Progress*.

Horace Walpole, *The Castle of Otranto*.

Clara Reeve, *The Old English Baron*.

Matthew Gregory Lewis, *The Monk*.

Anne Radcliffe, *The Mysteries of Udolpho*.

William Beckford, *The History of the Caliph Vathek*.

Rev. Mathurin, *Melmoth.*
William Godwin, *Caleb Williams.*
R. W. Emerson, *Works.*
Washington Irving, *Tales of a Traveller.*
E. A. Poe, *Tales.*
G. A. Bürger, *Lenore.*
E. T. A. Hoffmann, *Die Elixiere des Teufels.*
L. Tieck, *Geschichten.*
Victor Hugo, *Notre Dame de Paris.*

History and Criticism:

A. In General:

The Encyclopædia Britannica.
The Oxford Companion to American Literature. Oxford, 1941.
The Cambridge History of English Literature. Cambridge, 1908 ff.
—— *American Literature.* Cambridge, 1933 ff.
James Truslow Adams, *Amerikanskt epos.* Stockholm, 1939.
Wilbur L. Cross, *The Development of the English Novel.* London, 1905.
Klara Johansson, *Det speglade livet.* Stockholm, 1928.
Alice M. Killen, *Le roman terrifiant ou roman noir de Walpole à Anne Radcliffe.* Paris, 1924.
D. H. Lawrence, *Studies in Classic American Literature.* London, 1924.
Legouis-Cazamian, *A History of English Literature.* London, 1926.
V. Parrington, *Main Currents in American Thought.* New York, 1930.
A. C. Quinn, *Some Phases of the Supernatural in American Literature, Modern Language Association of America,* XVIII. Baltimore, 1910.
The Reinterpretation of American Literature, Ed. Norman Foerster. New York, 1928.
Helene Richter, *Geschichte der englischen Romantik.* Halle, 1911.
C. Van Doren, *The American Novel.* New York, 1921.
Van Wyck Brooks, *The Flowering of New England.* New York, 1936.

B. Concerning Hawthorne:

Henry Marvin Belden, *Poe's Criticism of Hawthorne.* Anglia, 1900.
Lina Böhmer, *Brook Farm and Hawthorne's "Blithedale Romance."* Berlin, 1936.
Elizabeth Lathrop Chandler, *A Study of the Sources of the Tales and Romances written by N. Hawthorne before 1853.* Smith College Studies, 1926. *Modern Languages,* Vol. 7. No. 4.
L. Dhaleine, *Nathaniel Hawthorne, sa vie et son œuvre.* Paris, 1905.
Neal Frank Doubleday, *Hawthorne and Literary Nationalism. American Literature.* January 1941.
Bertha Faust, *Hawthorne's Contemporaneous Reputation.* Philadelphia, 1939.
E. D. Forgues, *Nathaniel Hawthorne. La revue des deux mondes,* 15.4. 1852.

Julian Hawthorne, *Hawthorne and His Circle.* New York, 1903.

— —, *Hawthorne and His Wife.* Boston, 1884.

Henry James, *Hawthorne.* London, 1909.

Walter Just, *Die romantische Bewegung in der amerikanischen Literatur: Brown, Poe, Hawthorne.* Weimar, 1910.

John Macy, *The Spirit of American Literature.* New York, 1913.

F. O. Matthiessen, *American Renaissance.* New York, 1941.

Emile Montégut, *Un roman socialiste en Amérique* (*A Blithedale Romance*). *La revue des deux mondes,* 1.12. 1852.

— —, *Un romancier pessimiste, ibid.* 1.8. 1860.

Lloyd Morris, *The Rebellious Puritan.* London, 1928.

New York Times' Book Review, Two Studies of Hawthorne. Review signed Balakian. 25.6. 1944.

E. A. Poe, *Hawthorne's Tales.* Graham's Magazine, 1842.

Elisabeth Réti, *Hawthorne's Verhältnis zur Neu-Englandtradition.* Göttingen, 1935.

Leland Schubert, *Hawthorne the Artist.* Chapel Hill, 1944.

Anton Schönbach, *Beiträge zur Charakteristik Nathaniel Hawthornes. Englische Studien,* 1886.

Times' Literary Supplement, Nathaniel Hawthorne (unsigned). 3.5. 1928.

A. Turner, *Hawthorne's Literary Borrowings. Publications of the Modern Language Association of America,* 1936.

Wilhelm Veen, *Die Erzählungstechnik in den Kurzerzählungen Nathaniel Hawthornes.* Münster, 1938.

George E. Woodberry, *Nathaniel Hawthorne.* Boston, 1902.

— —, *Hawthorne, How to Know Him.*